GOING
CORPORATE

GOING CORPORATE

CORPORATE

MOVING UP WITHOUT SCREWING UP

BRAD EMBREE AND
JARED SHAPIRO

ST. MARTIN'S PRESS   NEW YORK

www.stmartins.com

Design by Phil Mazzone

Library of Congress Cataloging-in-Publication Data

Shapiro, Jared.
    Going corporate : moving up without screwing up / Brad Embree and Jared Shapiro—1st U.S. ed.
        p. cm.
    ISBN 0-312-33427-3
    EAN 978-0312-33427-7
    1. Business etiquette. 2. Office politics. 3. Office practice. 4. Interpersonal relations. 5. Employee orientation. I. Embree, Brad. II. Title.

HF5389.S53 2004
650.1'3—dc22

                                                                        2004048056

First Edition: September 2004

10 9 8 7 6 5 4 3 2 1

For Uncle Joel and Annette Soldinger

CONTENTS

CONTENTS

CONTENTS

CONTENTS

PART SIX: *CONGRATULATIONS, YOU'VE JUST BEEN PROMOTED*

CONTENTS

PART ONE

INTRODUCTION—SCHOOL'S OUT
FOREVER!

CHAPTER 1

YOU'RE HIRED!

CONGRATULATIONS! YOU MADE IT. YOU SPENT THE last four years staying up all night, drinking, screwing, smoking, partying, forgetting, screwing—and, of course, studying. Studying for what? Well, studying so you can get your first job in the Corporate World. Granted, some will opt out of that. Some may work in a small business with only three or four people, and some will go back to school to get their master's or doctorate, but at one point in everyone's life . . . you cannot avoid the inevitable. CORPORATE.

Let me be the first to tell you, there is absolutely nothing anyone can teach you in school about Corporate Life. There are no pie charts. There are no graphs, there's no research, no Venn diagrams, there's not even a handbook or a video (although some Corporate jobs make you watch a video during orientation that's more outdated than the "Red Highway" series you watched in Driver's Ed back in high school).

Hopefully, at some point you had an internship during your

college daze. If that's the case, you learned many valuable lessons—especially if it was a summer internship where you worked everyday for three months straight. Because that's where you learn the true lessons. If you're a guy, you've seen what it's like to be a boy among women. If you're a female, you've seen how older men act when they are away from their wives fifty hours a week. You've seen who's at the top, and you've listened to the complaints of those at the bottom.

Think of life as a big Ferris wheel with a different view from each level. You'll start to see now that things happen over and over again, and if you pay attention you can begin to learn from them. One day someone will ask you, "So what do you do?" You will be asked this for the remainder of your life. See, in college it was always, "What's your major?" And before that it was, "What school do you go to?" So get used to your new way of life because you are entering a whole new level.

"What do you do?" Some can answer "lawyer" and supplement that statement with ". . . but don't hate me." Some can say, "flight attendant," and some can say, "stewardess . . ." But rest assured, no matter what you tell people—they know EXACTLY what you do from your title. The trick is to present yourself in the most acceptable way possible because any idiot will immediately be able to judge what you do, where you work, and how much you make. Saying you're a lawyer is not the same as saying, "I'm an attorney." Don't just be a doctor, be a surgeon.

After a couple of weeks in the Corporate World, you'll know which newbie professionals pull in $24k a year and which ones pull in $36k. You might be the young woman who makes $24k—but if you give the illusion that you bank $36k, you'll get more respect. And respect is hard to come by; so if you don't give yourself your own props, no one will. Once you have respect, people will start relying on you, confiding in you, and, most importantly, they will let you rely on them.

But until you reach that plateau, here's the "skinny" on your paycheck: Let's say you make $35k a year. After federal, state, and local taxes, Social Security, Medicaid, company benefit plans (beware, this is where a company says you *get* benefits, but what it means is that you *pay* $50 a month for benefits), and anything else they can steal from you, you're left with about $27k.

Now pay your rent. If you live in a big city, your rent could be upward of $1,000 a month per person, but let's just say it's $800 per person: Throw in utilities, phone, cable, etc, and now you're up to around $1,000 a *month*. That leaves you with $15k. Doesn't sound too bad? Okay, now tack on a $100 a week minimum for food and you're down to $10k. Soap, shampoo, deodorant, cigarettes, drugs, and bar tabs are going to be $100 a week. Don't believe me? Look at your credit card statement after only one month. That late-night $79 tab from Maguire's Ole Irish Shebeen is a killer. That leaves you with $5k.

Transportation? This one is a biggie. Live in the city and you'll take the bus, subway, or taxi to the tune of approximately $5 a day. Lucky enough to have a car somewhere else, and it's $25 in gas a week plus the cost of insurance, and let's not forget oil changes, AAA, parking, and regular maintenance (i.e., replacing those brakes you've worn out completely from riding bumpers to and from work every day). All in all, you're forking over about $2,500 a year minimum, and this is assuming, of course, that you are driving a problem-free 1999 Honda Accord.

You buy clothes, maybe take ONE trip, buy music, see a movie or two (sans popcorn), buy presents, get a DVD player, haircuts, date a significant other for a few months during the summer, and at the end of the year—if you're lucky—you've got less than $500 to show for it! Depressing? You ain't heard nothing yet! Oh, and decide to keep that "significant other" around till Christmastime? Or, even worse, for a one-year anniversary? Good luck!

Now, if you're a woman—you have additional salary issues to

consider. You've got to eat, but you can't afford to go anywhere special. You'll see how quickly "Girls Night Out" will turn into "Girls Night In!" Moving on. Women like to buy clothes. And shoes. And purses. And accessories. After all, a perfectly coordinated wardrobe is an absolute necessity in the Corporate World. You don't see highly successful women working in major firms in major cities walking around in anything less than Chanel with perfectly coordinated Manolo Blahniks, toting a Fendi bag do you? Case closed.

Second only to the perfect wardrobe is the "other" necessity—hairstyling. Now unless you were born with the perfect head of hair, you're going to require a bimonthly regimen that'll include color or highlights, hair straightening or curling, in addition to the actual hairstyle. Women don't have their hair "cut," they have their hair "styled." There's a difference: $$$. You're also going to need a manicure, a pedicure, and an occasional facial. This is all part of the whole package of being Corporate. You know, the old "If You Look Better You'll Feel Better" myth perpetuated by the retail industry.

Presents. Gifts. Ah, the little "I Saw This and Immediately Thought of You!" pick-me-up gifts. Women love to buy gifts. Little presents. For any reason. Birthday, anniversary, retirement, wedding, new home, baby—if there's no "official" Hallmark occasion, they'll invent one. "Happy Thirty-third Day of Dating Day!" or "I Just Walked by Bebe and Didn't Buy a Thing Day"—so I bought myself a little treat!

Gifts that in the past were bought on a whim will now have to be carefully planned and budgeted for. Say "bye bye" to the Prada boutique and "hello" to Filene's Basement and discount bargain shopping. Bloomingdale's is replaced by Blue Light Specials. The rush you get from purchasing the perfect gift with absolutely no regard to how much it costs is now gone. It's yours again, *once* you make it to the top! Motivation! Of course, when you get to the top, who'll have time to shop?

The Corporate job is a far cry from your summer job carrying bags at the Radisson or waitressing tables at Applebee's. In college you used to read *Rolling Stone* and *Cosmo*. You arranged your classes "around" your favorite TV shows. You watched *Jackass,* the *Simpsons,* HBO, and *Days of Our Lives.* But now your schedule is changing. The bands in *Rolling Stone* don't really interest you anymore and you already know the twenty sex secrets that drive men wild. MTV runs *Real World* twenty-four hours a day, you're never home to watch the *Simpsons* or HBO, and you don't even care if Stefano breaks into the mansion of Victor Kiriakis. There's only one show that you will be able to catch religiously, everyday, each week—The *Howard Stern Show.* And I'm not talking about the exploiting version on E!, I'm talking about the original show on FM radio. That's because now you're up every morning at 7 a.m.—and commuting!

Howard, I must admit, can get a little tiring. I probably only listen to him now about once a week, but for the first year of my Corporate existence, I listened to him each and every morning on the drive to work. I'd laugh my ass off at everything he said. And then one day while I was laughing at a joke on the air, stuck in traffic in the middle of Highway 405 in Los Angeles, it hit me. With my grin still on my face, I turned to the guy in the car next to me and saw that he, too, was laughing. And then I turned the other way and I saw an older woman laughing in her problem-free 1999 Accord. And then the rearview mirror. And then the car in front of me. And then my mind did a visual pan via a satellite camera from outer space, and as I zoomed away from the Earth in my mind I saw millions of people on the highways of America—all laughing at Howard Stern. And for the first time in my life, I saw my collared shirt tucked into my khaki pants, with my brown Bass shoes, and knew I had lost my individualism.

At some point you have to ask yourself why you are at work. Why did you go to college? Why did you get a job? Why did you choose the field you chose? Why do you get up at 7:30 a.m. and hit the shower, scarf down a granola bar and a little box of Tropicana, and head to work? Who knows, you could really dig the Corporate World. Even so, it still doesn't hurt to have someone (i.e., not your parents) give you practical advice on when to take lunch, what to wear, whom to talk to, whom to avoid, how hard to work, when to speak up, when to keep your mouth shut, and how to maneuver a promotion: all vital aspects of succeeding in the Corporate World. You can either climb the Corporate Ladder or walk underneath it, and what follows in this book is a series of instructions, guidance, and personal war stories straight from the frontline of the Corporate Battlefield. If you're a smart, likeable team player, you will rise quickly to the top. You will put yourself in a position to have others want to associate with you. And the ones who don't, you'll leave in the dust, even farther behind than they were when you started. Good luck!

PART TWO

THE BEGINNING OF THE END

CHAPTER 2

GETTING HIRED

Your Résumé

YOUR EMPLOYER'S FIRST IMPRESSION OF YOU WILL come from your résumé, so sometimes it's best to add a little color. Depending on the job, you may even need to exaggerate a little.

Since you probably haven't had a job that lasted longer than a summer gig or school internship, you'll want to stretch that June to August work period to May through September on your résumé. No one will know. If your future employers call your references, they'll stretch the truth for you. Note: Always have your references ready for the call. Hell, put your best friend down as a reference. Embellish a little. Or a lot!

If you choose not to list your friends as references, put some actual thought into who makes the cut. While you shouldn't have to do background checks for those esteemed individuals you list as your references, keep in mind that you don't know everything about them. Once I put down an old boss as a reference, and he was so happy to help that he actually called the place where I interviewed BEFORE they called him. When no one called him back, he called again. And again. My prospective employer called me and told me to please tell him to stop calling her. Needless to say, I didn't get the job. Nor did I list him again as a reference.

Prospective employers expect exaggeration. It's called creativity. It's probably how the person interviewing you got his or her job! If all you did at your internship was answer phones, but one time you actually answered phones for the president of the company, then say you answered phones for the head of the company! Embellish. If you booked a rental car, say you handled travel plans. Say you did everything. Make it look like you were hired for a learning experience; but while you were there you were thrust into the heat of the action, and they couldn't function without you!

I worked for the television show *Access Hollywood* one summer for an internship. My biggest responsibility was to drive the two hosts of the show from their offices at NBC to the actual stage where the show was filmed. Granted, I did various jobs around the office, but I knew that every day it was my job to gas up the old golf cart (fine, it was electric) and wait for the two hosts to come out. Sometimes I made one trip and took them both; other times I made two trips when they weren't getting along.

I was never actually assigned this job. One day I was returning from running an errand on the studio lot and the male host was running late and shouted, "Hey, can you give me a lift?" I said yes, rushed him to the stage, and then every day for the next three months, I showed up outside his office at the same time and drove him over. He loved it because it made him feel even more special, and celebrities love to have their egos stroked. Everyone on the lot saw him with his own personal driver.

When it came time for me to write my résumé for a future job, one of the duties I described for this internship was that I was "talent coordinator." I was. I "coordinated talent" to and from the set! When I was applying for my next job at the Marketing and Publicity Department at Sony Pictures, they asked if I had ever worked with celebrities or talent. Had I! *Access Hollywood,* baby; I was the talent coordinator!

When you send in your résumé, you have to make sure it is received. There are lots of ways your résumé can get lost in the mix—we're talking about Human Resources here. If you don't get any response at all within a week, give a quick follow-up call. E-mail is sufficient as a last resort; but keep in mind that e-mail doesn't require a response from a company. If you call and actually get someone on the phone, you can sometimes talk them into giving you an interview.

The fact is, if they're not interested then they're NOT interested. Most résumés they receive are all the same. And nothing—not designing, not color copying, not sending cookies, will get them to put your résumé on the top of the pile. There's probably an assistant, who for one reason or another decided to either toss or keep your résumé based on his or her own likes and dislikes. "Oh, I hate people that went to that school. Toss it." "Oh, they're from Fayetteville. Trash it." I know because I've been this person. I've thrown away résumés just because I didn't like a person's last name.

Don't feel bad about calling. Get someone on the phone; get an interview. While you shouldn't be overly friendly to the assistant who answers the phone, don't be rude either. Remember, that assistant's job is to answer the phones. And by calling in, you've just created work for them. Before you called, the assistant was probably busy checking out the vacation deals on Expedia, and now you've taken that away. You represent work. So make it simple when you talk to the assistant; just ask if they've made any decisions on the current employment opportunity.

If you follow up and still sense nothing happening, you can start to get a little more aggressive. Wait a couple of days and make a second call. In the end, 90 percent of the time you aren't even going to get that first call from them anyway. But by taking the initiative, you put the ball back in your court and while you may tick some people off, the sad truth is that you probably weren't going to get called anyway. And chances are they may even admire your persistence.

Last year I was put in charge of our internship program. I probably dedicated about fifteen seconds to this new task. When we were hiring interns, the person I hired was the one who called the most. When I didn't call her back right away, she followed up with an e-mail and a fax. She force-fed me her résumé until finally I said yes to an interview just to get her to stop calling. And then I hired her. I never even looked at her résumé. She got the gig because she took the initiative and made it happen. Oh, and the cookies she brought into her interview didn't hurt either.

The Interview

Being "Corporate" begins way before you're ever actually Corporate. It starts with the interview, which usually happens during your college daze. You have to take off your ripped jeans and sweatshirt in exchange for some nice threads. You have to shower, brush your hair, and prepare yourself for civilization. All of which, if you are still in college, are things you may not have done in a few years.

While you want your qualifications to set you apart, you also want your clothes to blend in. It's a perfect mix. Some places want you coming into the interview dressed in a suit—others want casual. Find out. Call an assistant there or, if necessary, swing by randomly one day and take a quick peek. If everyone there is wearing jeans and you show up in a brand-new suit from Bloomingdale's . . . you're going to look out of place. You haven't even started yet, and you're already letting them know you have no clue "how it all works." On the contrary, if you show up in a casual outfit from the

Gap or Banana Republic and everyone is wearing suits or nice black clothes, you'll also stick out.

Before going in for the interview, do some research. Go to Google.com on the Internet and see what's been said about both the boss and the prospective company. Get some background info. Also, know exactly how to talk, what to say, and how to say it. It's different at every company. Should you mention the new merger? I don't know. Should you make eye contact the whole time? I don't know. Wear white after Labor Day? Not a clue.

In terms of the actual interview, (1) get the interview first and (2) nail it by setting yourself apart. After the actual interview, say something nice to the secretary or office assistant. They usually weigh heavily in their boss's decision as to whom to hire. They need to like you. So make them. If it looks like they have a ton of work to do, leave them alone. They may not want to talk to you at that particular moment. Feel out the vibes and go from there.

Once you're in the interview, leave all your annoying ticks and habits at home. Don't crack your knuckles, bite your fingernails, chew gum, or play "air drum." Don't immediately ask about either vacation time or salary. Start off with something pleasant. Tell a woman you like her blouse. Flatter her. Be straight with a guy. Talk sports if you notice his trashcan has a basketball hoop. Bring them down to your level; don't necessarily try to come up to theirs! Make them feel hip and young. Tell them how exciting you are, what you do, what you bring to the table. Don't tell them you were secretary of the Key Club. Who cares!

Who to Work For—Battle of the Sexes

Be wary of whom you want to work for. Decide whether you want to be working for a man or a woman because it will be a huge part of your Corporate happiness. Some of the time you may not have a choice, especially in a tough job market. But if you are deciding between a few job offers or find yourself in high demand for some reason, perhaps you'll get the opportunity to choose. If you are lucky enough to have a choice, give it a lot of thought because ultimately it will affect not only the longevity of your tenure but also your Promotion Potential.

Your Promotion Potential is a variable that can change by the hour, week to week, or month to month, and depends on every aspect of your Corporate performance. By dressing right, showing up on time, and hanging with the right people, your bosses will take notice of you and the promotion will come faster.

You want bosses with a high Promotion Potential because, whether you like it or not, for the next year you will be riding their coattails. If the ride is bumpy, you're in for a long, frustrating year. Always ride out the storm because if they are focused, they are successful, and up you go! If they move on, you move on. You're part of their success, and some of it—no matter how little—will be shared. If your bosses are going nowhere, all you will ever see is your tiny paycheck—no matter how hard you try. And if the company isn't making any loot, you won't see anything at all.

When you walk into the office of a prospective boss, look around. You're a forensic investigator, and this is your crime scene. With a sharp eye, you will know everything you need to know in a matter of seconds. There are important things to look for that will offset your risk and tell you a lot about your Promotion Potential.

Does your immediate boss wear a wedding ring? Is there a picture of the family or spouse in the office? If so, how is it placed? Is it on the desk just facing your boss or is it on the credenza behind the desk facing you? If it's there for the whole world to see, that's a good sign; the boss showing off the family. If it's only facing the boss—bad. That means he or she doesn't want you to see the family. Big red flag. Maybe there's no picture of any family. Maybe your boss is single. If so, will your boss always be thinking about love? Will your boss's focus on the job be somewhat distracted? Don't work for someone who's distracted. That lowers *your* Promotion Potential.

Some of you may prefer to work for men; some may prefer to work for women. There are pros and cons for each, so it makes sense to examine each scenario separately so you can choose which way you want to go. After this, I think you'll see that your best option is to work for a Pat.

FEMALE NEWBIE WORKING FOR A FEMALE BOSS

This combination usually works out pretty well; but when it doesn't, the downfall is often due to superficial nonbusiness factors. Is the boss attractive or not-so-striking? Either way works, just understand what her attractiveness means. It could mean your future. Then again, if she's ugly, she could be really smart and nice. That works! But she could also be depressed or perhaps kept down by the system. Not good for you. You can't take the time to worry about this or it will turn into something that keeps you down as well. This is your career after all. If you wanted a charity case, you would have applied to be a teller at your local food bank.

If she's attractive, maybe she's also smart, then she's got two things working for her. But then again she could turn out to be just "arm candy" with no brains, or she could possess a bad reputation for being "loose." In the end, no one is going to respect her, and, therefore, no one will take you seriously. You'll be known as the young woman who works for that hot chick. Then again she could be gorgeous, witty, confident, and smart. And she could shoot you to the top in seconds: success by association. You're the ultimate power couple.

FEMALE NEWBIE WORKING FOR A MALE BOSS

In this situation it's almost better if the boss isn't too fond of the newbie. Everything will always be kept on a business level, things will run efficiently, and everyone will make out OK. But oftentimes the personal issues of the male boss will creep into this dynamic and things will fall apart faster than a Chinua Achebe novel. One male VP I worked with quickly acquired the nickname Boston Screamer because of the relentless way he would shout at his poor secretary. I later found out he wasn't on speaking terms with his daughter. This was probably his way of showing that he was still in charge.

Sometimes male bosses won't care about actual job performance. Perhaps they'll simply like the female newbie because she reminds them of a new girlfriend. Male bosses will act very protective in these situations and bend over backwards for the female newbie. This is great for Promotion Potential; the newbie can do no wrong. This works both ways, however, as I've also seen newbies who remind bosses of their ex-wives. These newbies never had a chance.

MALE NEWBIE WORKING FOR A MALE BOSS

This relationship isn't all backslaps and extra seats to sporting events. Is the male boss married? If so, is he the type to cheat? If so, can you trust him to help you with your career? Is the boss part of the "club" that will allow him to get promoted, or is he just pretty good at what he does, so he'll always have a job but never really make it to the top?

In this situation your success can often depend on trivial things that are totally out of your control. Say your boss is a sports fan. He is guaranteed to be in a bad mood if his teams don't make it into the Super Bowl or World Series. If you're lucky enough that his alma mater gets into a big bowl game, but then they lose, it's all coming down on you. Then there's March Madness—if you show even the slightest interest in sports, he will ask for your advice when he's picking his brackets. Don't mess this up; you'll never hear the end of it. Especially if he bets money.

Male bosses often tend to look to male assistants to validate their masculinity. They're jealous that you haven't blown out your knees yet or that you can still swing a golf club. It'll be you they'll turn to when they need a dose of testosterone. They'll see a picture of a woman in a bikini, and all of a sudden, they're your frat brother. Trust me, you don't want to be that guy who has to talk about sex with a fifty-year-old stranger who has the ability to fire you.

MALE NEWBIE WORKING FOR A FEMALE BOSS

Being a guy, my experience with women—albeit older women— was basically limited to family. I quickly learned that the women in the real world are nothing like the women in my family. Women in the real world are CRAZY. Hey, women, guess what? Men in the real world are CRAZY, too. So there, everyone is CRAZY.

The fact is, people say things for a reason. So let's examine some of those "things." First of all, prejudge all women the second you meet them in an interview. Don't prejudge *all* women—just the woman with whom you are going to be serving for forty-five hours a week for the next year. Size her up. Is she married? Is she dating? Is she divorced? Does she have kids? Is she rich? Is her family alive? Is she pretty? Long hair? Short hair? What are her interests? Hobbies? Old? Young? Gay?

Notice one thing: these are all personal issues. Notice I didn't ask about or point out one part of her work character. Because it doesn't matter! Women at the workplace are who they are because of their personal lives. If she isn't married . . . she might be looking. If she's old, she wants you to be young for her. If she's divorced, well—all men are assholes. If she has kids, at least one part of her has a "motherly" instinct, but don't be so sure it will carry over to the office.

Let's sum it up. Women are equal to men. We know that. But in the workplace, unfortunately, women do have a disadvantage because men are, for the most part, in charge. Qualifications aside, often women are judged for other reasons. People in the workplace know that when a man is mean and hard-nosed, he's just "the Boss." But when it's a woman, she's labeled a "bitch." It's a completely unfair stereotype, but it's a fact.

Men are judged on a different criteria. Is he gay? Does he want to watch baseball with you or does he want to "play" baseball with you. Are you a guy? Are you a woman? Is this guy doing what the rest of his family does? What did his dad do? Is he the same religion as his boss? Does he dress well? Does he drive a nice car? In the end, will he get promoted? If he won't, neither will you. These are ALL things to consider. What you take from them varies from each person depending on who you are. Are you a guy? Are you a woman? Do you prefer to work for someone of the opposite sex? Do you want to work with someone of the same sex?

Remember that ultimately it's your immediate boss who's going to help you succeed. Want a raise? Want to get promoted? It's your boss who's going to let you get there. Notice I said "let." Because you will get yourself there, but ultimately he or she is the one who has the final say. If you're lucky enough to have a couple of job offers, definitely consider who you want to work for before you accept any of them.

Your Corporate Identity

 The Corporate World is a tricky one. You are no longer surrounded by family. You are no longer surrounded by friends. You are no longer ever left alone. You're at work. Got that? You're going to spend more time at this place than you do at home. You're going to see your coworkers more than you see your parents, your spouse, your friends, your girlfriend, your boyfriend, your dog, yourself—because you will spend a minimum of forty hours a week with these people. To survive, you'll need to establish your "Corporate Identity."

At first you may be able to hide your true identity. If you're a huge party animal, a pothead, an alcoholic—at first you'll be able to conceal it. "Hey, Jim in Marketing is a pretty cool guy," they may say about you. But a month later, you'll crack. At a company function someone will dare you to do a shot. And you do. Ten times. Someone will have a joint. So you'll smoke it. A coworker will ask you to go to a strip club. Or Happy Hour. Or to take an extra thirty minutes for your lunch break (sad, but when in the Corporate World, taking thirty minutes extra for your lunch break is the equivalent of going to Happy Hour. Or a strip club.) And you'll do it. And all of a sudden you've strayed.

It's important to check your personal baggage at the door. It's a new world. Come in with a clean slate. Forge a new identity, a better "you." If you were the slut in college, if you were the pothead in high school, if you were introverted, if you were a gossiper—leave it all behind. Right now, on your first day of work, understand that you are just another employee, a walking Social Security number that receives a direct deposit for two weeks' worth of hard work.

In college there were all types of people doing all sorts of things. But now that's all changed. There's nobody with dreadlocks. There are no nose rings, no loud stereos, no dyed hair. It's all been replaced by computers, suits, and talk about the weather. The water bong has been replaced with the water cooler, and the only high you'll ever get at work is when the elevator is going up.

Your mom or dad told you the night before your first day at

work to "just be yourself." Be yourself? Okay. Go to work wearing only your underwear and tanktop, drink milk out of the carton, sit on the couch and watch TV. That's *yourself,* right? So there, you see, the very first piece of advice you ever received was wrong. <u>DON'T be yourself.</u> The trick is to be someone else. Someone Corporate. Be Mr. or Miss "I-love-work, I'm-really-fucking-good-at-it, I'll-stay-an-extra–half hour–tonight, goddamn-we-work-for-a-great-company." Be that person, at work. Then go home and sit in your underwear and tanktop, and drink milk out of the carton in front of the TV. It's all you'll have left at the end of the day. You can now be yourself.

Be a myriad of different people in your Corporate Identity. Just be. Get by. Excel. The goal in the beginning is to fit in, make money, and find out what's right for you. Look at everything as a new experience. Because it is. You may think it's a cinch doing this work thing. Because it is. The work itself is easy. You'll see what I'm talking about in a few years. The work itself is easy. It's the bullshit that's hard.

Having a strong Corporate Identity will help you develop important life skills. Since you now work close to fifty hours a week, your "self," as you know it, is evolving. If you spent fifty hours a week pumping iron, you'd be ripped. If you spent fifty hours a week running, you'd be in incredible shape. If you spent fifty hours a week cooking, you'd have Wolfgang Puck eating out of your unwashed hands. By spending fifty hours a week as a "worker," that worker mentality rubs off on you. If you are aggressive and persistent at the office, it will transfer to your life outside of the workplace. If you don't take "No" for an answer at work, you will be less likely to lie down when someone is trying to walk all over you.

Act Mature

Maturity is the most important aspect of your soon-to-be-established Corporate Identity. It's called "acting mature" for a reason. It's all an act. When you go to work, you look different, you dress different, you even talk different. You're not yourself. Even if you have the maturity of a month-old 401k, you must act mature at work for one reason and one reason only: your future.

Your coworkers will not take you seriously if you run around the office like a twenty-two-year-old, rubbing your youth in the face of the executive down the hall. It's great that you still have close friends and fresh college memories to keep you happy. But put yourself in the shoes of the thirty-seven-year-old junior vice president down the hall who's been doing for fifteen years what you've been doing for fifteen days. He's not as happy as you, not quite as chipper, and certainly, while the office may be your playground, this guy has mortgages, car payments, and his children's college funds to think about. Immaturity will only antagonize him, and you may need his help in the future.

Acting mature is an acquired skill. In fact most of the bigwigs hanging around your office probably deserve Oscars for the emotionless facade they display week after week. They've had years to master the act of maturity, and they've been reaping the rewards ever since. In a decade, however, these bigwigs will be a thing of the past, so let's look at the future.

Let's say Jim in Marketing has been working two years longer than you. While you're just figuring things out, he's already got his entire route mapped. Jim's experience is not necessarily a bad thing. In fact it's OK that's he's ahead of you for two main reasons. In the future, Jim might be your boss. He's going to be due for a few promotions before you even get your first one, and if he sees that you're an up-and-coming newbie with a mature attitude, he'll be more likely to put in a good word to the Head Boss.

There's also the chance that Jim might leave the company for a better gig that offers him more money and a better title. And when Jim leaves to head up another department, he'll be making staffing decisions that could directly benefit you if you've acted maturely throughout your brief tenure working with him. If Jim is looking to bring over some fresh recruits, rest assured that if you've played your cards right, you'll get poached faster than an egg in a fully comped Las Vegas buffet. The last thing you want Jim to remember is the time you filled the whoopi cushion with sulfur and placed it on his secretary's chair when she sat down. No, you want him to remember the nicely dressed, well read, mature new employee who, if given a chance, might be a mover and a shaker before too long.

At this point you have options. Even if you want to work with Jim at his new endeavor, consider the fact that Jim's recent desertion also leaves open additional responsibilities at your present company—and if you've acted the part, you could be just the person to move up to Jim's slot. So stick around for now. Jim will call you if he needs you.

I'm always amazed by the older, more experienced executives who don't understand the importance of maturity. I used to work with a senior-level executive one of my bosses hired. Only three months into the gig, he left for an even better job at another company. The manner in which he quit was immature, and it left a sour taste in my boss's mouth. So nine months later when he found himself out of a job because of cutbacks, who did he come crawling back to? His boss. And just to spite him, his former boss offered the guy a job one notch below where he had been. Now the guy had to choose whether to suck up his pride and take the job or just let it go. Well, he let it go. And I later learned that the boss knew the guy would NEVER take the lower job. But he figured he'd offer it anyway. Why? Because he was the boss. And that was the mature thing . . . for a boss.

Decisions: The End of Thoughtlessness

For the first twenty-one years of your life, everything you did was of little consequence. Sure there were decisions that at the time might have seemed like everything was riding on them. But decisions like "Should I lose my virginity on prom night?" or "Should I drive my car after having two beers?" are nothing in the grand scheme of life when you consider what's ahead of you after college.

Consider that, for the most part, your pace on the treadmill will forever continue to slow. Every sexual partner you meet could be "the one" rather than just a random hook-up from a college bar. And now the chances of meeting someone in a bar and bringing them home only to find out they are a complete nutcase increases tenfold. These days, you don't want to crash your car—but not because your parents will be pissed, but because your car insurance will go up. Smoking pot in your room now might land the cops on you—not school security. A bad performance at work could get you canned, and that's not the kind of C you were used to.

It gets worse. Christmas vacation is no longer the entire month of December like it was back in school. Now, if you're lucky, it's the tiny window from Christmas Eve to New Year's Day. Summer is no longer two or three months. Now it's a three-day vacation on Memorial Day and again on Labor Day. Every five years or so July Fourth might fall on a Friday or Monday, and you can stretch it to another three-day vacation.

Life also becomes increasingly condensed as important decisions confront you. You can't just get bombed one night and sleep through class—you've got to be accountable for the 9 a.m. meeting with the Marketing Department the next morning. Everything you do from here on out will require thought, a moment, and a reconsideration. Should I go to that concert on Tuesday night? Should I do one more shot of Bowman's Vodka (it is midnight on a Wednesday after all). Should I kiss this guy? Is she "the one"?

Should I get in my car and floor it? It is mine now. Being able to hurt your own car shows you how much you've matured since you were a teen. The difference between now and then is that now you are held accountable for the consequences of your decisions. Get used to it.

THE BEGINNING OF THE END

The Importance of Your College Transcript

Ok, so now you see the importance of your college transcript.

CHAPTER 3

SHOWING UP

The First Day

BEFORE YOU WALK INTO THE OFFICE ON YOUR First Day, think about one thing: from here on out the only person on your side is you. Sure, your friends and family are there for you when you need them; but honestly, on your walk into work and when you get on the elevator for the first time, your friends and family aren't going to be there (which is probably a good thing unless you want them to see you cry). If you're insecure; if you think you're ugly; if you think you smell bad; if you think you're dumb, inferior, or inexperienced; if you think you're anything less than capable and ready, it's going to be a long, tough road. Your enemies will eat you faster than a box of See's Candy.

Your company hired you because someone thought they needed you. But when you show up at work for your First Day, most of your fellow employees will see you as more of a hassle than anything else.

You're going to struggle your first few weeks there. People are going to talk about you, say bad things, hope that you fail. That's OK. It's just like your first day of school as the new kid or like rushing your fraternity or sorority. But you survived that, right? Here's what you can expect:

After you wait for a good ten to fifteen minutes in the lobby, someone will finally acknowledge that you have no idea what's going on, you have no ID to get through the doors, you have no keys, you don't know where your desk is, and you don't know what you're supposed to do once you find it.

An assistant or office manager will come over and take you to your desk. You'll get a five-minute pep talk from this person, even though you will later learn that this is probably someone that no one else likes, isn't very capable, and is very low on the totem poll. That's because all the capable people pass the work down, asking someone else to take care of you. The good people are busy. So that leaves this person, whoever he or she may be, to do it.

This person will explain that you get an hour for lunch and tell you where most people go to eat, when they stay in, what's good, what's bad, as if you have the same exact taste as everyone else. This person will turn your computer on and tell you whom to call to get your e-mail working and whom to nag to get your ID badge. Of course, nothing will ever be set up prior to your arrival. Efficiency never matters.

Now it's an uphill battle. And a test. You have to get on the phone with IT (that's Corporate for computer geeks). They'll hook you up. Next, call Security (translation: thugs who failed their police tests), and they'll get you your very own ID. Once you're officially "activated," you'll get a quick rundown of how the copier works, you'll be told whom to call with certain problems, whom "never" to bother, followed by snippets of who's nice, who's mean, who just got divorced, who's promiscuous—all the relevant gossip.

Take it all in—this is actually very important. At no other point in your tenure are you ever going to be given so much background information on ANYTHING. And yet here you've been at work a whopping thirty minutes, and already they're providing you with everyone's bio. Listen closely, this will come in handy later. Also keep in mind that they are all sizing you up too, from the second you walk in.

There's an inevitable moment that will undoubtedly be the worst ten seconds of your first day. This happens when you attempt to join in on your very first conversation with a clustered group of coworkers. You'll see them talking, and they'll be talking about something you can relate to. So you speak up, injecting a nugget of information into their conversation. Maybe you'll even say something that will include a little fact about yourself so they can start getting to know you. "Yeah, I saw Beck play during college back in Virginia Beach."

No matter what it is you choose to say, their reaction will always be the same. They will all stop talking and stare at you like you're some sort of alien. This will be followed by ten seconds of complete silence until one of the coworkers breaks the silence with a nervous laugh. Don't worry, this is the same for everyone. It happened to them on their first day, it happened to you, and it'll happen to the next newbie they bring in.

Eventually you'll get the standard interrogation from your coworkers; it's your Corporate Initiation Test. "Who hired you?" "How much are you making?" "What city are you from?" Some will feign interest in your hometown, and then you'll have to play the Name Game. No matter what city you're from, this coworker will automatically assume that out of a city of five hundred thousand you'll know their friend, ex, college roommate, prison penpal, whomever. And maybe you do, and then this person will say, "Wow, small world," and just like that you've formed your first corporate bond. You're well on your way.

Your Desk—Finding the Happy Medium

Whether you have your own office or you need GPS to find your cubicle among your coworker clones, someone else was sitting at your desk before you, and that someone else has left their mark. It's that person's rubber band ball or their paperclip snake link in your drawer, even though you add to it. Maybe it's that person's unused napkin, which one day might save you from a spill, or it's his or her paperweight on your folders. Regardless, it's always going to be that person's dirty dust in each corner of the drawer and his or her handwriting on all the files. It may be awhile before it actually feels like it's your desk.

As someone once said, "If a cluttered desk is the sign of a cluttered mind, then what is the sign of an empty desk?" And that also goes for your desk at the office. Like everything in the Corporate World, you need to have a happy medium. You don't want a sloppy desk. A sloppy desk indicates you are lazy, unorganized, and irresponsible. But most importantly, it's unprofessional.

However, if your desk is completely empty, clean, and tidy, that means you don't have enough work to do. It tells others you're not important. It says "anal" and "too much free time." You shouldn't have time to keep your desk area clean all the time. It should be something you do once a month, so people notice it. "Hey, you cleaned up your desk," they will say. And that means they noticed. You want people to notice your desk has tons of stuff on it. Not trash. Just tons of files, papers, pictures, documents, proposals, spreadsheets, mail, messages, Post-its. "Hey, you've got a lot going on," they will say.

The most important thing to remember about the happy medium is cleanliness. Just because you want the appearance of being busy, you don't want cookie crumbs, ketchup stains, or old bottles of murky water sitting on your desk. A plant might be nice, but that could show too much of your soft side. Buy a plant and then let it die. It shows you tried. And in the end, isn't that what matters?

Whatever you do, don't overdecorate or incorporate any kind of themes. Go look at the Senior VP's office and then go look at the VPs' offices. The Senior VP is where you want to be, and aside from a few family photos and an autographed Mickey Mantle photo, he's all business—because guess what? It's his OFFICE, not his playpen. Now go back to the VPs' office who just got a "pity promotion" after eight years of service. He hangs the invitations from every party he's ever been invited to on his bulletin board. That Laker Girl he met, you'd best believe there's an autographed photo hanging on the wall. The promotional Koosh Ball he got at the networking convention is hanging from his corner halogen light. DON'T BE THIS GUY. You're at work, not redoing the door of your dorm room for second semester.

Getting the Chair

The electric chair probably provides more comfort than whatever chair they make you start off with. The chair that is at your desk on your First Day is the worst chair in the office. Odds are, if there was a good chair there from the previous person, someone else pilfered it and replaced it with their shitty chair before you were hired. Go out and seek the best chair you can find. The whole floor is yours now: find that new chair; find something that works for you. If you find a chair that has armrests, for example, they need to either slide over your desk or be low enough to slide under the desk when you scoot all the way up to your keyboard. Factor in the small details because you're going to be stuck in this chair for ten hours a day for the rest of your tenure.

There are two types of chairs you should press for. One is the ergonomic chair that adjusts around your spine to maximize comfort.

They are expensive though, so if your company won't spring for one of those, look for a chair where the back goes up to the middle of your spine. This is the perfect spot for the ultimate back crack. This chair is a chiropractor's wet dream. A couple of times a day you can lean all the way back in your chair, your spine will crack and pop, and for a second, you'll know what heroin feels like.

On some chairs you can control the height at which your chair stands, and this says a lot about you. You don't want to be too high—you'll look like a tyrannous monarch overseeing his empire. You also don't want to be too low or you'll look like a lazy slouch. Sit up straight and keep your chair at a decent level: high enough so that people respect you; low enough so that you're comfortable.

Love Thy Computer

Check out the computer on your desk and immediately begin considering options for improving it. Chances are it has the memory capacity of a ninety-five-year-old man. Try and get the best computer available for whatever job you do. If your job involves anything creative, you may want to explore the offerings of the Mac. For all else Corporate, a PC is the way to go. When selecting a computer, the most important thing to realize is the age of your computer. Your company may try to stick you with an old model that they had in storage rather than spend a grand on a new system with the latest Windows software. You want to make sure your computer is new and fast and can support the latest music-downloading programs.

There are a couple of ways to check the age of your computer. First, look at the mouse. Does it have one button or two? One-button mice are older than the Rats of Nimh, and you can't do anything right if you can't "right click." The newest mice actually come with a nice little roller ball that lets you scroll around on the screen with ease. I get so accustomed to using this feature at work that I come home at night and try to scroll on my home mouse even though there's no roller ball. It looks like I'm petting it.

Another easy way to check the age of your computer is to open the Spell Checker and type in the word "Internet." If it doesn't get flagged, start downloading your favorite songs. But if your computer doesn't recognize that key word, your biggest thrill will be the chance to beat your high score in Minesweeper. But never play Solitaire. That's a lonely man's game, a sign of weakness. Plus, your boss will kill you, especially if you're coming close to his or her high score.

Benefits

Don't be fooled by them. Sure, they're good for cocktail party conversations. It's always good to lift eyebrows by reciting the huge benefits package your company has bestowed upon you. But too much boasting at company parties only means less time you get to spend eating pigs-in-the-blanket, and how many times a year do you get the chance to chow on those? Besides, the day that sitting underneath fluorescent lights and staring into your sun-glare computer monitor ever actually "benefits" you is the day you qualify for worker's comp and a 401k power plan.

Companies often entice newbies with long-term benefits that don't really factor into the life of a young adult. Life insurance, disability insurance, retirement plans, child care, you're going to hear them all. At some of the more generous companies, they may even give you an office with a window so you can see everything you're missing on the outside. Newer companies usually offer more benefits. I wish my father's company offered child care, then I wouldn't ever have to find a job!

Whether you carry a purse or a Proton Pack, a good company should always offer you health-care benefits. But what they don't tell you up front is that in order to qualify for health care, you have to first get a physical. This is typical of any corporate job—two days in and they've already got you bent over a table. It's only a sign of what's to come.

A couple of years ago they made me schedule my physical for the Monday after Super Bowl Sunday. I considered myself to be fairly healthy, but it turned out I had more problems than the guy in the board game Operation! Ten hours after I'd single-handedly eaten enough nachos to affect Taco Bell stock, I had a nurse asking me why my cholesterol levels were off the chart. The nurse who tapped into my vein somehow managed to find some blood in my cheese stream.

Sometimes your company may try and entice you with a health club membership. This only translates to more time you have to spend with your coworkers. You DON'T want to be a part of your company gym, no matter how nice it is. The gym is the place you're supposed to escape to when you want to relieve stress. Will you really find it relaxing when Jim from Marketing hops on the elliptical next to you and starts talking about the latest expense report? If you don't have time to go to a gym outside the office, just eat a bag of veggie chips. Those things are like exercise-in-a-bag.

In the end just take your damn benefits and cash in on the fact that for $10 you can roll up to the chiropractor with a serious case of *workback* and get thirty minutes of blissful body cracking and realignment, courtesy of the corporation that put you in this horrible physical and mental state in the first place!

Morning Efficiency

The morning has a snowball effect on the entire day. Getting ready, eating breakfast, looking nice, smelling good, feeling good, etc., are all important factors for your Corporate Identity and Promotion

Potential. You could be a great worker and highly intelligent, but if your clothes are wrinkled, if your breath stinks, if your face is oily, if you're tired, if your body has an odor, it will totally overshadow all the other positive attributes you display.

Take care of all that stuff early. Pick out acceptable clothes and make sure they are clean. Don't wear stained clothes; you'll regret it all day. Don't wear wrinkled clothes; use an iron for five seconds. Don't wear anything too short or tight. Be well groomed. Tuck yourself in. Perfume and cologne are fine, but avoid overpowering scents that enter the office before you do.

Getting ready in the morning is all about multitasking. Remember, the quicker you get ready in the morning, the longer you can sleep. Do two things at once. Brush your teeth while you are relieving yourself. Gargle with mouthwash while slipping on your socks or looking for your wallet or purse. Do things that need to be done sitting down together. Do things that need to be done in the bathroom together. Have an order. Do the same thing each morning. Figure out what takes too long and shorten it—or eliminate it. Wash your hair at night if you have to. Get out of your house with a minute to spare—maybe even five.

Do everything quickly. Don't turn on the TV. Get up, get ready, get to work. You'll get home earlier at the end of the night because of it. If you're an early riser—if you've previously been labeled a "morning person"—you've got it made. You may not even need coffee to open your eyes in the morning. Beware, you will have very jealous coworkers, and they will manifest themselves over the coming weeks.

PART THREE

ACCLIMATION

So you've been at it awhile. The first couple of weeks have gone by, and for the most part, you've got things figured out. "Corporacana" isn't so bad, you may tell yourself. People are starting to learn your name, your ID badge is working, and your benefits will be kicking in any day now. You've got a good desk, a nice chair, and a decent computer. For the first time since you started working, you feel satisfied.

But don't! This is only the beginning, and you should never be satisfied. It's time to start climbing that ladder to success. Become a part of the team, while at the same time keep your distance and look out for yourself. Your instinct will tell you to do things your way. Why should you blindly trust a bunch of strangers telling you how things work. What do they know? You're teeming with ideas and suggestions that are going to propel you to greatness in record time.

Well, slow down. Before you can change anything, you have to first know how things are currently being done. Then, and only then, can you bring about change, put your spin on things, and leave your signature.

CHAPTER 4

THE DAILY GRIND

Monday Mourning

I HATE SAYING, "GOOD MORNING." IT'S ONE THING to say, "Morning" or, "Hello." But it's a completely other thing to say, "Good Morning." It's not good. It's morning, but it's more like *mourning*. I would say, "Good Mourning," if that's how they spelled it. But they don't, so I just say, "Bad Morning." What? It is.

Monday morning undoubtedly is the worst part of the week. The weekend came, the weekend went, and it's back to business. Same people in the elevator, same white hallways, same person standing over the coffee machine in the kitchen, same fluorescents, same glare on the computer monitor. And what makes it all so unbearable is that it's now time to greet all your coworkers again and say your "good mournings."

It's time to pretend that you care about what happened to them in the forty-eight hours since you saw them last. You can't let this get to you, you have to override the impulse to walk past your coworker with the fresh cup of coffee, past the white hallways, back into the elevator, and back to your home pod. Monday Mournings are easiest if you swallow your pride and actually get interested in the lives of your coworkers. Think of their lives as mini–soap operas. If Fridays are the cliff-hanger, Monday morning is Sweeps Week. Did Kevin confront his neighbor about that pesky tree branch that needs clipping? Did Samantha work out that thing with her cell phone? The trick is to find someone who actually did something worthwhile over the weekend. The bigger your cubicle farm, the more interesting stories you will uncover.

You can also perk up your Monday morning blues by spicing up your greeting. You don't always have to say, "Good morning." Try something new: "How are you," "How's it hangin'," "How you doin'," "What's shakin'," "What's up," "What's going down?" Spice it up by throwing out a "Como estas." But not with a Boss! You want to be taken seriously. You not only say "Good Morning" to a Boss, but you follow it up with a, "How was your weekend?" And you say it sincerely. Because you mean it. ☺

Monday Mourning may be when your thoughts are the darkest, but you can also use it as an interesting way to track your progress in life. I try to view Monday Mournings as a fresh start to a new week. The sun is shining and the body is rested and ready to be fueled up for the daily grind. This line of thinking may come naturally to you, but with some, the good feeling ends within seconds. With the first glance out the window (if you have a window), you realize that a good 50 percent of the year doesn't start off with the sun shining.

Mondays are the worst day of the week because chances are you were out late over the weekend and most of the time your body isn't rested from a good night's sleep. You probably hit the snooze button an extra time and didn't have time to eat breakfast, so you end up going to work after swallowing a Centrum and a gulp of stale water from the cup you poured last night.

I remember driving to high school in the tenth grade. Maybe in the rain. I would get to the parking lot early in the morning and want to stay in my car listening to one last song before I ran off for a long day of doing things I didn't want to do in a place I didn't want to be. Don't get me wrong. I recognized school was a valuable tool—I understood that fully—but I still didn't want to be there. I wanted to wait in the car. I sometimes thought I would rather sit in my car, even with the music off for eight straight hours, rather than actually get out, walk to class, and start school. Eight hours of nothing vs. eight hours of unenjoyment. You decide.

Every once in a while, the Corporate version of this memory comes into play on Monday Mournings. I ride up to work in the elevator, thinking to myself, "I'd give anything to have this elevator break down in the middle of two floors right now. I'd be stuck here all day. And I'd love it." Eight hours of just hanging out in a metal cube, hearing only a fireman asking, "You all right in there, buddy? We'll get you out soon!" I'd say, "Oh, I'm fine. Take your time. Please don't do anything to jeopardize the situation. Be safe." And I'd wait all day. Deep down everyone in the office would be so jealous. Because we were all trapped in cubes that day, the only difference was, mine was sealed off from the rest of world. It would be the best morning ever. I'd have to deal with no one but me—and the fire chief.

The Restroom

Before I started my first job, one of the smartest lawyers I've ever known gave me great advice about efficient use of the office restroom. "The office bathroom is like your cell phone. Never use it before 7 p.m."

The restroom is the most challenging part of the work atmosphere. Sure it's only a small fraction of your day, but its impact can be instrumental in your acceptance into the Corporate World. Think about it. When you're at home, you close the door to the bathroom so that your roommates or your boyfriend/girlfriend doesn't hear you. Now imagine you're at work and there are two other stalls next to yours and you've really got to go. You go in, sit on the toilet, and suddenly a boss or one of your coworkers walks in and decides to brush their teeth or brush their hair for three minutes while you sit there. It's not fun.

If the cubicle farm is the "war zone," the restroom is "home base." It's the one place where normal rules of society don't apply. Five minutes after your CEO chews you out in his office, you could find him talking sports in the urinal next to you like nothing happened.

And chances are your CEO will find a way to test your mettle. See what you're really made of. Be prepared to hear the nastiest fart you're ever going to hear in your life. Be prepared so you don't laugh when you hear it. Of course five minutes ago, when he's ripping you a new one, he wouldn't have dared to rip a squealer this bad. But it's home base, it's the safety zone, and he knows you're not going to tell anyone. Telling someone would seem juvenile. Even if you did, who would believe you?

You have to be careful in bathroom situations because you don't want to be labeled. I knew a guy at work who was labeled *"El Diablo del Baño"* (the Bathroom Devil). He was a marketing director—had a pretty solid job for a huge TV production company. And yet all of that went down the toilet, literally. He had no idea people called him by this name. The problem was, this guy had no shame when relieving himself. He would just go into the bathroom stall, pull down his pants, sit, and release nuclear winter upon all of those innocents just washing their hands or putting in their contacts. The smell was like nothing you have ever experienced.

People always assumed he just ate a lot of spicy foods, but there were plenty of people in the office, and no one even came close to doing the long-term damage El Diablo did. No matter how hard he worked, this guy would never go anywhere in terms of a promotion with an unofficial title like that. And coworkers are evil—remember that. They spread the word fast. It became a stigma around the office for him, and he never even knew it. You didn't want to talk to this guy, eat with him, or even shake his hand. He had been labeled unsanitary. He had been labeled, *"El Diablo del Baño."*

Over time getting up to use the restroom will become an exercise in avoidance. Sometimes you'll spot someone that you don't want to be with behind closed doors. No matter how bad you have to go, you'll hold it in. You'll walk right by the restroom pretending you're going somewhere else. Then you'll take the long way back to your desk and sit and wait another hour before attempting to go again.

The really weird thing is that other people feel the same way. Someone might see YOU on the way to the bathroom and decide that he or she doesn't want to go in while YOU'RE there. They, too, will just keep walking as if they were headed elsewhere. Then, of course, if you do the same thing, neither of you will end up there. Then there are the times when you sit on the toilet and wait for people to leave before you flush and go. This is to avoid talking to them or sometimes to avoid having them know that it was you who just dropped that stinker.

If you get stuck in a stall, keep an eye out for shoes in the bathroom. If you get bored, you can see if you can recognize people by their shoes. I like playing "the Bathroom Memory" game. If I see Vans, I know it's the mail guys. A nice pair of Ferragamos means someone important has entered home base. I'm sure it works the same across the hall; just look out for the Jimmy Choos.

Oftentimes a person will enter the bathroom the same time as you. You go into the stall and pretty much just sit there quietly, hoping someone will flush or turn on the sink, anything to make noise that will conceal what's about to go down. Maybe you use the Preliminary Flush. But then the person who walked in with you (whose face you saw also) will make the loudest, most disgusting noises, as if no one else is around. That person will proceed to go at it for a good minute or so, moaning, groaning, and then giving a sigh of relief. Then he or she will get up and wash his or her hands and just sort of smile at you. Do they not realize that you could tell everyone what you just heard? Remember El Diablo . . .

That's not to say you're perfectly sanitary. From time to time you have gas. Every one gets gas at the office at some point. You spend at least eight hours a day at the office; surely you will get gas. Saturdays and Sundays you get it, but you're in the friendly confines of your own house. You can pass it at your leisure. But what to do at work?

Maybe you have a cubicle out in the open; maybe you have the luxury of your own office. But even if you do have your own office, you can't very well let one fly whenever. Someone could walk into your office seconds after you let one go. It's not worth the gamble. The dilemma is even worse if you're in a cubicle farm because then you're surrounded by coworkers all day.

So you need to establish a safe house, places where you can go to let off a little steam. Your first thought, naturally, would be to head to the restroom. But you probably already go to the bathroom two or three times during the course of the day. You don't want to go into the bathroom every time you have gas. You'd be making ten trips a day. Your coworkers would see you going in and out of the restroom all day long. And you can't have that. You can go into a closet, but again, that's risky.

The place with the least risk is the copy room. It's well ventilated because of the heat generated by the equipment, and this minimizes your trail. But each office is different, so plan accordingly when finding the most practical safe house. As you get accustomed to your office surroundings, isolate several safe houses. Chances are some may have already been compromised by another newbie who's been there a couple of weeks longer than you.

E-mail

Remember when your friends actually had faces, and not just e-mail addresses? E-mail has now replaced the phone conversation, especially in the corporate environment. It's the voice mail of the Information Age. Fresh out of college, you're probably well immersed in the world of e-mail. I came out of college when e-mail was just hitting it big, back when no one had a clue what the "BCC" button did.

Times were tough when I started my first job in 1999. Remember Y2K? Imagine spending the first year of your job having to hear a bunch of bearded executives running around the office telling you that at the end of the year every computer in the office was going to magically stop working. That's when I realized for the first time that all my superiors were idiots and something had to be done. But that was way back in the twentieth century.

Five years ago, there wasn't really an understood code of ethics on how to execute the starting and ending of e-mails. Someone would write me an e-mail, and I'd write them back immediately. Then a few minutes later my computer would "ding," and I'd see they had responded to my response. And this could go on for five or six e-mails, of, "Thanks!" to, "No problem" (or if the person feels comfortable with you they will write, "No problemo," or, "Ciao").

E-mail is your way out. If you really wanted all of that toppings bullshit, you could have either called the person or handwritten a nice note. Instead you e-mailed them so you wouldn't have to talk to them. So send an e-mail; don't waste time playing little communications games!

When someone sends you information you requested, be wary when you say thanks. Sometimes it's necessary. If you send out the information and the other person says "Thanks," just let it end. Don't be the "no problemo" guy. Let it end. It's really no different than the prerequisite phone conversation of, "Hey, how are you doing?" "Good, how are you doing?" "Good." Then, "Great, I'm calling because . . ."

If you are writing coworkers at the same level as you, you can be very casual with them. You don't need to sign your name at the close of each e-mail because your name is already there at the top of the page. They know it's you. You can even just end it with a "Thx" instead of a "Thanks." Things like that are understood.

If you are writing your boss, however, the rules are different. Check that puppy like it's your taxes. Do everything properly, no lowercased letters, no abbreviations, make sure you use Spell Check, and polish up your grammar. Anything less would be like talking slang to them. And this is indicative of your work in general. Make your e-mail a work of corporate art—nice, neat, to the point, and exactly what they were looking for: an answer to their question.

One important thing to remember about e-mail is that it's proof. And that can work for or against you. Phone conversations are air. Someone can *say* they said something, but in the end if there's no proof, it might as well have never happened. E-mail is different. If someone writes that they are going to take care of something for you, or they provide you with information via e-mail, you'd better hold on to that information like it's gold. It could be your get-out-of-jail-free card!

If there is a fuck up, you can always refer back to the e-mail that Jim in Marketing sent you containing the wrong information. You just send it on to whoever is accusing you of the problem and say, "Attached is a copy of the e-mail Jim in Marketing sent me on January 12, 2002 (treat it like it's a court case; your guilt or innocence is on the line here). If this information is not correct, please let Jim or me know so we can correct the problem."

The fact is you don't want to screw over Jim. That's not the issue. All you've done is let the powers-that-be know that it wasn't your fault something went wrong. But you *and* Jim are willing to rectify the situation. In the end Jim's best hope is that the same shit happened to him and hopefully he saved the e-mail.

Your Corporate e-mail also becomes an extension of your Rolodex. Rolodexes of the past used to contain addresses, zip codes, job titles, and other info that has since been rendered useless. Because now you e-mail. All you need is a name@company.com and you're set. Over the course of a year, many people are going to send you hundreds, if not thousands of e-mails with people's contact information, statistics, facts, names, phone numbers—anything. And because you are at work and most likely are bored and lazy, you won't actually take the time to jot down this information and put it in your Rolodex. You won't take the time to actually print it out and file it because you've made a mental note that it's safe in your e-mail.

In fact it probably is. You'll always know it's there, as long as Jim in Marketing doesn't open that suspect-looking virus e-mail that will erase everyone's hard drive. But you're already miles ahead of Jim. You don't open e-mails with titles like "Big Worm" and "Trojan Horse."

Make sure you erase any incriminating e-mails from your hard drive. Any X-rated e-mails you received, look at them, hold on to them for a couple of days, forward them, do whatever—but ultimately, GET RID OF THEM. Don't ever write anything too dirty, gossipy, racist, or sexy in your e-mails. The idiot on the other end could show it to someone, accidentally reply to someone else, keep it up on their screen unknowingly while they go to lunch—or, worse, they could be sick one day and someone else could be using their computer. The last thing you need is a temp clicking through your hard drive and finding a photo gallery of two co-eds going at it in their dorm room.

Always remember to carefully read over what you are sending out. If it's something that could hurt you down the line, don't send it. It's not worth it. If you're working for a big company, they can watch your every move. They OWN the computer, and technically you are working on THEIR time. They can Big Brother you however they see fit. Contrary to popular belief, your company has EVERY RIGHT to spy on you. Ask any lawyer. Or better yet, send an e-mail to an imaginary Hotmail account from your corporate e-mail talking about bombs, murder, drugs, and corporate espionage—then see how long it takes before Corporate Officials come running over to you. Just kidding. Don't ever do that until you're sure that all seven numbers you picked in the Powerball Lotto are 100 percent correct.

Over the years e-mail has formed a language of its own. Things haven't been the same since some loser with too much time on his hands made up the word "emoticon" and then figured out a way to communicate using parentheses and semicolons. Don't be the ":)" guy. Internet smiley faces were cool when they first came out, but now you really only need them if there's a chance you may have offended the person you were writing. You can say, "Damn, Cindy, isn't that the same outfit you wore yesterday? What did YOU do last night?! :)" Internet smiley faces soften the blow and sometimes even allow you to make a couple of cruel jokes because you know you can tack on an Internet smiley face and all will be forgiven. "Your report was the most worthless piece of crap I've read all year. :)" See, the smiley face makes it all better! You can use them more frequently if you're a woman because then it makes whatever you're saying sound "cuter," like the "XOXO" signoff. "Don't hate me for taking the last diet Dr. Pepper :)."

Every so often you'll have a karma e-mail exchange and do a favor for someone who doesn't work in your office. Someone from a random company will call up and somehow end up with you on the phone. You're not exactly the person they should be talking to, but it's not like they're asking you to solve the world's hunger problem—so you help them out. Maybe they need you to send them something via FedEx or they need you to find an answer. When they contact you via e-mail, make sure you save that e-mail. Three or four months from now you are going to need something from them. And when you do, you'll have their e-mail to "reply" to. As a reminder of who you are, keep the same subject heading of whatever the original message was. It says, "Hey, remember when I helped you out? Well, now it's time to pay me back!" And it's all good because they'll know you helped them out once. And now they'll help you. It's the start of a beautiful relationship.

Coffee

There's a simple test to see if you will ever turn into a coffee drinker after college. It goes like this: HAVE YOU EVER SEEN AN ADULT WHO DOESN'T NEED A CUP OF COFFEE IN THE MORNING?

In college when you had your own schedule, coffee wasn't a necessity. Sure, some of your friends enjoyed a daily dose, but no one ever drank it because they HAD to. Maybe there was a time when you had to speed through the *CliffsNotes* of the book you were supposed to read two weeks ago. Maybe you started frequenting the corner Starbucks to impress the Goth Kid from your English class. Regardless, it was never out of necessity.

After college, however, you have to be up early every day of the week. You have the responsibility to be at certain places at certain times. You have become Corporate. So let's face it, as you get older, coffee becomes increasingly routine. Coffee is habit forming: it's the drug of the Corporate World.

There's a coffee machine in every office, and this isn't an accident. Coffee is a great way to get the morning started. It makes you feel more alert, and this will make it easier to deal with the Anderson account that was due two weeks ago. Coffee is overabundant because your bosses want you to drink it. They want you to get hooked. Maybe they even offer to buy you one on occasion. Don't mistake this gesture for generosity. They're simply dealing you a brown liquid containing chemicals that make you more productive.

What they don't tell you is that it also makes your heart beat faster than it should, and oftentimes it even upsets your stomach. To the bosses you're nothing more than a machine. You've left your pod for the day to perform mechanical work to make money for them. Coffee is their way of speeding up the machine. Don't let them get you!

Distractions

When I'm at home and I try to sit down and do some work or read or anything constructive, I always end up turning on the TV. I'm the same way at the office, and since there is no television, sometimes I have to find my distractions elsewhere. Corporate distractions are all over the office, and for the most part, it's important to eliminate them if you want to do a good job at your bad job. Start by getting rid of any and all games on your computer. Minesweeper, Solitaire, Hangman, Tic-Tac-Toe—get rid of them all. I had a coworker who played computer games all day. He even participated in Internet games and tournaments. I would walk by his desk to say "hi" and he couldn't even tear his eyes off his screen. Even when he answered his boss's phone, it was one hand on the phone, one hand on the keyboard. He was obsessed. And two years later, while everyone else had been promoted, given raises, or moved on to bigger and better jobs, he was still at the same job, dominating poker-people.com. And he didn't even play for money.

If you are distracted at work, your coworkers will notice. Even the sneaky ones get caught because it's simply not something you ever grow out of. I worked with a VP who always complained about how busy he was. He seemed stressed every time anyone talked to him. People just assumed he was a hard worker always focused on his job until a coworker walked past his office one day and noticed that she could see his computer monitor off the reflection in the glass window behind him. She saw that he was working on a nice game of solitaire. In fact he never stopped playing. Turns out he was never stressed. It was all an act so he wouldn't have to work. He had all of us fooled. Not only did he spend his days playing virtual cards . . . he had been playing us as well. The funny thing is, we all knew about it but no one ever said anything to him, so it was a constant source of amusement whenever this VP would give us the stressed-out routine. Who knows, I bet he's still out there somewhere, dragging the red ten over to the one-eyed jack.

The biggest Corporate distraction is Instant Messenger. You don't need it; it's simply a luxury. An evil luxury. It's the least constructive way to spend your time. In the beginning of my Corporate work experience, I stayed logged on to Instant Messenger (IM) all day. I knew I was wasting all my time, but I couldn't help it. It was so much better than doing work. Now that I'm a wizard of all things Corporate, I've afforded myself the luxury of IM so that I can maintain contact with a couple of people. That said, I only log on for a couple of minutes a day. I DO NOT keep it up and running all day.

If you feel like you must have IM to make it through the day—at least keep it off most of the time. Otherwise you'll spend all day on it. Not only is it bad for you to be so distracted by it, but you also don't need other people walking by and seeing you IM'ing your buddies. It looks bad. I had a coworker who used to keep his IM on all day. He'd have seven different conversations going at once. All his coworkers knew he did it, and everyone knew he was the biggest slacker.

IM almost got me IF (instantly fired) when our Human Resources Department circulated a memo stating that all instant message software must be removed from the computer by the end of the day. Apparently profits were down, and the bigwigs were concerned that some of my coworkers (not me of course) were using this program to chat with relatives and college friends.

Most of us just laughed off the memo. We IM-ed a couple of one-liners back and forth, wondering whether people would actually take it seriously. Sure, there were several white collars and a couple of communists who immediately laid down and called IT to uninstall the software, but most of us understood that it was Human Resources after all, and after the actual circulation of the memo, their job was done. They could care less whether we actually did it, we were not affecting THEIR bottom line. In fact most of them probably gave out the memo and hurried back to their office to go IM their relatives and college friends.

After the memo made the rounds, I logged onto IM a couple of minutes a day, and no one suspected a thing; but one day Corporate Murphy's Law was not in my favor, and as soon as I logged on, the president of the company came running out of his office to look at a file. He was standing right behind me and one of my college buddies must have seen I was online. Suddenly, my computer made a beep, and a single message popped up on my screen; "What's up, fuckface?" I turned red and looked around. The president was looking down at me. He shook his head and told me to answer the question.

The Commute

During a cab ride home a couple of months ago, I realized for the first time that riding in a New York taxi is exciting when compared to the rest of the day. Then again, after sitting in a chair staring into a computer monitor for ten hours straight, anything would seem exciting. I can only imagine the excitement commuters in exotic parts of the world must feel when riding home in a rickshaw.

Driving is another sign that proves you hate work. If you have your own car, the first thing you do when you leave work is floor it. You get in that car, you pump the music as loud as possible, unbutton that shirt, and screech out of the parking lot. You're free! Go!!!!!

Believe it or not, even your taste in music will change during your commute. It used to be that you always had music on. You were always lounging around because your next class didn't start until after lunch. But now that's all changed. Now listening to music might only exist for the twelve-minute drive to work and the thirty minutes you're stuck in a traffic jam on your way home after work. Driving to work you'll want to listen to something that really "flows" because it's a fresh new day and you want to groove and hear something good. On the way home, though, you've got all of that pent-up anger and aggression and you just want to rage! You feel differently now. What were you doing playing Dave Matthews this morning? That wasn't you; it's certainly not what you're feeling right now. So on the way home you blast the loudest rap or metal you've got.

After a few months you'll notice you don't listen to any of your favorite CDs anymore. Why? Because the drive home from work is no place for Nirvana's "MTV Unplugged in New York." Somewhere along the way your "Appetite for Destruction" became an appetite for NPR.

You are better off if you're in a city where you can walk to work. Walking to work is like traveling abroad. Remember when you came home after a month of bland foods and no water pressure? All of a sudden you land in America, and all you want is a chalupa and a hot shower. When you leave work for the day, you'll have spent too much time in a sterile, white, empty atmosphere of an office.

All day staring at a computer monitor. All day sitting in a chair. All day with your hair neatly groomed, all day being proper! And then you're walking home, and you hear that saxophone player on the corner going to town on his brass piece. At first you're still in office mode and you pass by not hearing a thing. But then you remember, "Wait! I'm human! I hear the sax player! And he rocks! This is really good!" And then you almost throw him some change. Almost. Hey, it's not your fault your company doesn't pay you more!

Weather and Traffic

I read a study that said most Corporate workers talk about the Weather and Traffic so as not to actually have to confront any true thoughts, emotions, or feelings with their coworkers. I agree, I don't think you should get too personal with your coworkers except in the case of your bosses. Then it's fine to get as personal as necessary, and if they get personal, too, that's all the better. Your bosses may view you as a person they can talk to because you know what's going on in their lives, and they also know you're not supposed to talk to anyone about what you discuss. When your bosses start divulging personal info, it's best to keep your ears open, your mouth shut, and, depending on the topic, a look of either interest or compassion on your face.

Most of the time you will find yourself in the elevator or walking from the parking lot when the Weather and Traffic talk begins. First it will be the Weather. You'll talk about the temperature—hot or cold—and then you'll get into specifics. Talk about the humidity, the rain, the wind, and everything else that goes along with it. Now ask yourself—do you read books about Weather? Do you regularly watch *The Weather Channel?* Do you even know any weathermen? No. So why are you talking about it?

Then you get into the topic of Traffic. You'll complain about it or maybe you'll say "Hey, traffic wasn't so bad this morning." Because what Traffic and Weather represent are two subject matters that all workers have in common. What no one realizes is that there are tons of other subject matters you have in common, too . . . you just don't want to talk about them. You all have family, dying relatives; you all like sports, movies, music, and fashion; you all have cavities, root canals, blisters, eye problems, heart burn, impotence, an abusive boyfriend, loud neighbors, a sick dog, stolen cable, diarrhea, no dishwasher, a friend in jail, or a failing relationship. But are you going to talk about any of those things? No! Of course not! So talk about this morning's gridlock because that's always fun!

On that first day at work, when you get on the elevator, or when you're walking into your office—LISTEN. If the things people are talking about aren't the Weather or the Traffic, then throw this book away. Throw this book away because everything I say is untrue. But if you hear people talking about how the Weather is nice, or how all it does is rain, or how it's supposed to be nice all weekend, get your best Traffic one-liner on standby. That's the next order of business.

Dress Code and the Casual Friday

Don't let Sprite™ fool you, Image is EVERYTHING! Your image directly impacts both your Promotion Potential and your Corporate Identity. And nothing creates your image better than your wardrobe. Your clothes are the first thing everyone will notice from the moment you step off the elevator.

Put some thought into your wardrobe so that it looks like you didn't put any thought into it at all. Create an image around the type of work you do. You have to dress for the position you want, but a little bit above it, and a little bit below it. Case in point, if you are an assistant to a high-ranking executive, you need to dress very professionally. Everything should be clean and neatly ironed. If you are young, however, you have to remember that one of the reasons you were hired may have been because of your age—your hunger and your freshness. Therefore, don't shop at Men's Wearhouse or Ann Taylor for your clothes. Head over to Armani or Marc Jacobs. If you can't afford it, check the Marshalls's clearance section. Sure the pants may have a third leg sewn in, but hey—they're Kenneth Cole!

While you want to be professional, you still need to be trendy. It will make your bosses think you are hip and fresh, and they will like associating with you—it will make them feel like they have the "cool" assistant. However, you don't want to dress too hip. Guys, don't wear an earring, don't dye the hair, and keep the facial hair scruffy at most—clean shaven on Mondays and for important meetings. Women, look your best, wear earrings. Show off what you've got, but don't go overboard.

There are the occasional dress code events that you DON'T want to participate in. These are themed dress days. They tell you to wear green on St. Patrick's Day or red on Valentine's Day. Don't do this. Again, by participating in themed dress days it shows you are consciously thinking of what you are going to wear outside of the office. It shows you have a "home" and that you are not a machine. You want to give the impression that you are a machine and that your home is just the pod where you go to pick out your snazzy black garment. You shouldn't own anything red or green for work anyway. I'm not talking about the abolition of colors—colors are happy—I'm just saying let's remember you're at work, not the carnival.

Most important, don't participate in Casual Friday! It's the totally wrong way to express casualness. Nothing looks more stupid than trying to be too casual at work. Case in point—guys tucking their button-down shirts into jeans. You're not a preppy at an oyster bake. In order to be "casual," you actually had to think about the jeans and the outfit vs. just wearing what you usually wear. Therefore, it wasn't so casual, rather it was more prepared. Real Casual Fridays would mean feet up on the desk, music blaring in the background, and leaving your cubicle to finally go chat it up with that striking young professional on the tenth floor.

CHAPTER 5

EXTRACURRICULAR ACTIVITIES

Corporate After Hours

CORPORATE ACTIVITIES COME IN ALL DIFFERENT disguises, and some may even sound like "fun." A Breakfast Staff Meeting. Our Annual Company Picnic. The Christmas Party. None of these will *ever* be fun. Think about it. Where would you rather be: playing Secret Santa or in Victoria's Secret?

Make no mistake, these are all Corporate Activities. If it was a fun activity, it would read something like "Lounge on Your Couch from 2 p.m. to 6 p.m. This Saturday." That's what you really want to do. But instead, there will be activities like "Potluck Lunch." Be careful of these. You don't want to seem like a party pooper, but you also don't want to be totally into these things. You don't want to slave over a spinach and artichoke dip all weekend. It looks bad. It says to others, "I didn't have anything better to do over the weekend than cook potluck food." Besides, if your meal actually turns out to be good, they're going to want you to make it every time.

So participate, but only volunteer to bring the sodas. Spend the extra five cents to buy the two-liter bottle of Coke or Pepsi, not Private Selection or Sam's Choice . . . no matter what you may drink at home. Don't go all out, unless of course the Head Boss is really into these sorts of things. If he or she is, usually it will be in the form of a specialty dish, and you have to pretend you can't wait to stick your fork into his or her marinated duck medallions. If this is the case, spread your wings and make something nice to go along with it.

While you may have to participate in a potluck, never attend any company events scheduled at a beach. If you live near a beach, chances are it's your most relaxing getaway spot and should therefore never be mixed with anything Corporate. If you have friends of your own, go with them on your own time.

If your coworkers plan a Happy Hour days in advance, don't go. Don't be fooled. Granted, sometimes you are going to land a job with really fun people that you can relate to. If that's the case, it won't be a planned outing where the time and date are scheduled in advance and blocked off on the company calendar. It should just be something you all do spontaneously.

The Christmas Party

This is the closest your life and company will come to a Reality Show. This is gloves-off, no-holds-barred, hard-core reality. There's no computer for you to turn back to when you're done talking to one of your coworkers. Unless of course your office party is at work—and usually that's just in the movies, like *Die Hard*—where the employees worked and had their party at the top of Nakatomi Plaza. But, hey, if you had an office like that, complete with a waterfall, you'd probably want your party to be there, too!

If your annual Christmas Party is held outside of the office, chances are it's because your predecessors previously held one too many wild after-hours parties at the office, thereby necessitating the need for a change in location. It's a well-kept Corporate Secret that office equipment becomes fun when under the influence. Booze, when mixed with a Xerox machine, leads to the circulation of photocopied boobs and butts. And imagine all the drunk dialing you can do on a phone with fifteen lines!

The Christmas Party is like going to a huge party where none of your friends were invited. In fact the party is so unusual because of the people who ARE invited. This is the one time you get to meet everyone's better half. All year long you've been hearing about the spouses, fiancés, boyfriends and girlfriends, and it's finally time to put a name to the face. Of course, the only reason they are invited is to reduce the risk of potentially embarrassing situations.

While you may enjoy meeting all the people you've been hearing about for months, know that they've also been getting an earful about you. They actually have the upper hand because they're the ones who know if their significant others like you. You can learn a lot about your coworkers if you notice how their significant others greet you.

You may actually be looking forward to finally meeting these illustrious folk. But don't get too comfortable; you're liable to stumble across the one who likes to talk about his or her sex life. You have enough stress at work; you don't need a visual image of Barbara in Human Resources going at it with her beer gut husband. Delete those images from your mental hard drive.

The Christmas Party is a bizarre event, and it's important to remember that whatever happens, your bosses will still be your bosses the next morning. So be careful. Those needing to succeed will find it high time to dress nicely for this festive occasion so as to impress their bosses. The nerds who never go out will drink two cosmos and totally embarrass themselves. The good-looking youngster that everyone thinks is gay will finally prove that he really is. The woman who is rumored to do coke will do coke. The guy who always cheats on his wife will cheat on his wife. The fat guy will follow around the appetizers waiter. The cheapskate will steal extra party favors. The cool chick will show up late. The moms will go home early. The bosses will give speeches and leave. Everyone will clap.

Then later, a wasted underling will give the real speech and thank the real people. The party will wind down, and you and the few people you like will be looking for a place to go for the *after* party. Some people will suggest a shitty place. Let them go there while you and your peeps go somewhere else. The 10 p.m. closing time of the Christmas party will soon turn into a 3 a.m. curtain call full of excitement and memories that you may or may not remember in the morning.

The Christmas Party can change everything. You can climb the social ladder or improve your Promotion Potential over one Jack and Coke—or you can plummet with just one shot of Bacardi. It's up to you. There's no learning curve on this one. You're either the fat guy who follows around the waiter or you're not. You're either the cokehead or the straightedge. Make the right decisions and perhaps Santa will bring you a promotion.

Birthdays

Similar to the Christmas Party, the Potluck Lunch, and wearing green on St. Patrick's Day—the Birthday Party can be awkward. First and foremost, pray your birthday is on a weekend. That way you get to spend the day with family and friends. Problem solved; disaster averted. Unfortunately, the odds aren't in your favor.

When your birthday occurs during the workweek, you have to decide whether or not you are even going to announce that it's your birthday. Someone will say, "Good morning. How are you?" And you can respond with, "Pretty good. It's my birthday. And you?" It's best to just slip them a hint a few days in advance. That way it won't be a big production, and half of your coworkers will forget anyway because it's information that doesn't involve them so they're not interested.

Don't let everyone take you out to lunch or dinner for your birthday. Say no. Sneak off if you have to for lunch. Or go with one, maybe two people. But don't make it a mini–Christmas Party at the local Denny's with the whole staff. If they get you a cake, be calm and collected. Enjoy it, but don't be totally into it. Remember, having a birthday makes you human. You are a machine! A working machine! And the Boss is still watching you.

Be careful of your birthday enthusiasm when it's someone else's birthday. Lots of companies will pass around a card for everyone to sign. When signing a card for someone, be careful what you write. The Head Boss will be the last person to see it, and he will read all the messages. So don't write anything incriminating, sexist, or alcohol-related. Say something kind of funny. Write "Happy Birthday!" and sign your name.

I know a lot of people who take off work on the day after their birthday. This is just about the worst message you can send to your boss. It screams that you're a disaster. "Hey, look at me. It's my birthday and I'm going to get so wasted tonight that come tomorrow, I won't be able to perform menial tasks in a Corporate environment!" Toughen up, this isn't Day Care.

Drinks

After working a few months, a new form of socializing will enter into your life. Partying goes to a whole new level when you join the ranks of the Corporate World. It used to be that you would just go out and get wasted. When your friends called, they'd ask, "Want to go out? What are you doing tonight?" In the Corporate World, binge drinking is replaced by a new form of social event—one that you will do for the rest of your life. DRINKS. Yep, it's called DRINKS. "Wanna meet for drinks?" "Let's go get drinks." "We should do drinks sometime." "We definitely have to do drinks."

Maybe there's that girl you call on the phone two or three times a week for business. One day you make her laugh or you're thrown together on a stressful project, and then—Bingo! It's completed and you can finally relax and you say, "Hey, we should DO DRINKS sometime."

What exactly is DRINKS? Well, DRINKS is when you show up to a bar separately to meet someone you've never met before. You get there first and usually wait at the maître d's podium or hang out at the bar drinking a water or you wait outside talking on your cell phone.

Anyway, when your DRINKS partner finally shows up, you'll decide whether you want to sit at the bar or grab a booth. You'll say the prerequisite, "It's really great to finally meet you." Then you'll both order drinks and start chatting. You'll chat about work, your bosses, where you each went to school, your personal lives, your coworkers. Then you'll order a second drink. It's at this point that the game begins. Because after that second drink is when you'll determine whether the night goes on or whether you walk back home with your head held down in shame. If you're on to drink number three . . . That could be a good sign.

Be careful who you get DRINKS with and watch the information you choose to disclose. Sometimes after an eventful day at the office, one of my bosses would suggest that we walk up the street and grab a drink. This is a great way to get to know your bosses, and it reinforces that you're doing a good job. Have drinks with your bosses whenever you can, but make sure you watch what you say. By the time their glass is half full (or half empty, depending on whether you had a good day), chances are they'll try to get you to start talking about your job. "Off the record," they'll say. It's easy to say something you may regret in these situations. Don't mistake a boss for your friend and start complaining about your salary. There is a time and place to do this, but it's not the Happy Hour at the Shebeen.

Women should watch out for the guys who are more shallow than the water in the water cooler at the end of the day. Never tell a guy you're single unless you're prepared to change the entire focus of the conversation. And keep in mind that a client is still a client. And if you're the client—remember you're the client. Also, remember it's not good to fish off the company pier—you don't want to go out and get wasted and hook up with someone from your office.

Corporate Dreams

Usually they come on Sunday nights. Every now and then you may fall asleep and have a Corporate Dream. In between the good dreams, the ones where I can fly or play a guitar, something Corporate slithers its way into my subconscious; and I have a dream that I'm at work. I've had dreams where I had to load a Xerox machine with an endless supply of paper. Others, where I've had to deliver a message to a boss by sprinting across the city in the blinding rain. Usually I'm just stuck in an office that looks like a Fritz Lang movie.

Corporate Dreams are tough to shake off. I hate waking up from them in the middle of the night because they make me bitter about my job. It doesn't seem fair that it's 3 a.m. and already I feel like I'm at work. It hurts so much that I should be getting paid by Worker's Comp each time I have one. All day long the bigwigs abuse my physical body, and now they own my subconscious mind, too? It's frustrating but it's just one of those things that comes with the Corporate territory. You spend the majority of your week there, so naturally you're going to dream about it.

CHAPTER 6

LIFE ON THE FARM

The Cubicle Farm

CUBICLES ARE MOUSETRAPS DISGUISED BY COM-
puters and fluorescents; and like those stupid business books will tell
you, everyone around you will try and "take your cheese." "Good
fences make good neighbors," as Robert Frost said, and you need to
set the precedent as soon as you enter the farm. You don't want your
coworkers entering your air space every five minutes, but you also
don't want to give off the Unabomber recluse vibe either or you'll be
left out of everything, and not even the bosses (aka farmers) will
trust you. When initiating a conversation, it is always best to use
safety zones such as the copy room, vending area, and kitchen.

Everyone hears everyone's conversations in the Cubicle Farm.
If you're on the phone and talking to someone about something
fun or comical, you can be sure that the moment you hang up the
phone, whoever is sitting near you will make a quick comment as if

he or she were involved in the conversation. Your neighbor will add to the story, relate it to a similar one he or she had, or just add some icing to your little muffin of a story. If you are talking about something very serious or disturbing, however, you can rest assured your won't say anything.

It's impossible to have a moment of silence neighbor. Every phone call, heard. Every cough, heard. Every time you go to the copier, you walk past twenty people. Every time you go take a whiz, twenty people see you. If you check your e-mail, everyone sees you. Big brother isn't watching—the whole family is.

You need to be able to converse with everyone in the Cubicle Farm. It's good to have a mole in every department—that way you'll hear about the memos before they go out, you'll know what your Christmas bonus will look like, and you'll know what's cool to say around the religious guy. Making an effort to learn something about each of your coworkers' interests will serve you well in being known as a good person. It's almost as if you should be walking around with Post-its pasted on the walls in front of you constantly telling you to "Smile," "Be nice," and "Be courteous." All of those attributes will set you apart from the rest of the corporate drag. And that IS what you want. Otherwise you're just like everyone else. Take a look around the office—only about 5 percent to 10 percent get a promotion each year. Be in that percentage.

How to End a Conversation

One of the awkward things about being in a sea of cubicles is how to end a conversation. When you are seated at your cubicle, it's common to strike up a conversation with a coworker seated at another cubicle. Once you've finished talking, how do you go about ending the conversation when your coworker keeps on chatting? After all you can't just walk away, since you're both already sitting.

There's a right way and a wrong way to end a conversation. End it too abruptly and your action will be interpreted as rude. Prolong it, and your other coworkers will think you don't work as hard as they do. Either way you'll make an enemy. There's no point in talking, but it's yet another unfortunate part of Corporate Territory.

When a topic has run its course, you want to end it on a light note. Elevate your tone as you either make a quick joke or a reference to something you both will understand. "Well, if the landlord turned off her hot water, she should just use our water cooler!" You've acknowledged that you were listening to the story and also managed to get in a harmless office barb.

If that doesn't work, you'll have to use body language to speak for you. Position your hands and body toward your desk as if part of your body was getting back to work. Keep your head turned toward your coworker though and continue talking. Now that you've got your body busy doing something, you can fully turn around at the end of the sentence. This enables you to get back to work without offending the coworker. They will note your body language of getting back to business and will want to do the same. Remember, if conversations occur frequently or distract you, they will damage your Promotion Potential.

Conversational Guerrilla Warfare

Conversations are tough to end when you're in your cubicle. They're even tougher to end when you venture from your cubicle. When you're "on the road," you will see lots of other folks besides your two usual cubicle neighbors. One of the strangest parts about the office is the strategic maneuvering, the lengths you'll go to in order to hide from a particular coworker.

Say you're walking down the hallway and you see Jim in Marketing. You may stop and chat for a second, exchanging a couple of pleasantries and courtesy laughs before you go on your way. But ten minutes later you're walking down the same hallway and you see Jim again, only this time, for some reason, it's awkward. Neither of you have anything to say, the conversational topics have been tapped, so you both put your heads down and take a long swig of coffee just before you pass each other.

Think about how as a kid growing up in your home, you might pass a family member fifty times a day in your house. Going up or down the stairs—your older brother might hit you, your mom might kiss you, your dad might tell you to hold your shoulders up, your sister might nag you . . . but what about the fifty to hundred times you pass Barbara in Human Resources? You can't kiss her, and she's NOT going to hit you (though she *may* nag you).

So what do you do? You plot. You see her fifty feet ahead of you, headed toward the same copier as you. If you keep up your pace, you'll hit the copier at the same time she does. Slow down, she'll beat you. Speed up, you'll beat her. Make a left, you lose her. Make a right, you're in the kitchen. Stop and someone in the cubicle you're standing in front of might talk to you. But maybe that's a small price to pay. Conversational Guerrilla Warfare is an acquired skill that requires strategy and foresight to complete your objective of not having to cross paths with someone you don't want to see.

Skilled warriors subtly alter their pace just to change the eventual outcome of who they might pass along the way. They know that on the Corporate Battlefield there are bunkers, safe houses, death traps, air lifts, drop zones, and base camps. They use their given landscape. They use walls, podiums, desks, shelves, rooms, windows, elevators, doors, and/or other objects to escape.

You may run to the back copier just as much as Chatty Andy over in Research runs to the laminator, which just so happens to be on the same path. And if you don't have any sort of relationship with him (other than passing him ten times a day in the hall) it will just be plain old weird. It's not like after four months you're going to stop him one day and introduce yourself. Speed up or slow down when you see him coming. Make a turn when you don't need to. Stop at someone's desk. Head into a closet. Or better yet, don't get up at all. Stay at your desk all day, and have an intern do your copying for you.

Who's in Charge?

As you continue to get acclimated, some of your new coworkers will try to assert their power over you, but after a few weeks you'll realize they are nobodies. The office can at times be one big power struggle. People who get treated like shit in the real world figure that maybe at the office they can throw a little weight around. Let these people know they are severely mistaken. Learn the hierarchy and apply it as soon as possible.

For instance, in the entertainment industry, a development assistant might hold more power within a company than the Director of Research in the same company. One might be twenty-four years old and making $31,000 and the other might be forty years old and making $80,000—but it doesn't matter. Everyone knows the development department is in charge, and an assistant there is going to wield more power. Same goes in any company. Figure out who's in charge and go with it.

Don't let people boss you around because they most certainly are going to try. Don't let anyone make you feel inferior. Your coworkers are going to assume that because you are young and somewhat inexperienced in the world, you don't know much. They're going to be talking with one another about politics and current events, and they won't include you in the conversation. The only time they will even look your way is if they can't think of the name of that song by the newest trendy band.

Don't take it personally. They have the problem not you. In fact I'd go so far as to say you are more knowledgeable than they are on virtually any topical subject. After all, you might have just gotten out of college and taken four years' worth of classes that dealt with the subject at hand. Whether you appreciate it or not, you are more learned in politics and international affairs than you think.

People at other companies will try to boss you around over the phone. If you're calling someone to ask for a person's number and they respond with "That person doesn't work here anymore," don't just say thanks and hang up. Ask them for that person's contact info; or if they don't have it, ask to speak to someone who might have it or talk to that person's replacement. Get what you originally intended to get. Don't let someone else steer you off course.

A lot of times you are going to have to call people or e-mail them asking for a favor or for some information. Don't be apologetic. Don't be, "I'm sorry to bug you," or, "I hate to bother you," when starting off. First, you should never give them that power, and second, what the hell are you sorry for? You're at work; you need the info—they are at work; they have the info. You're both doing your job. Don't act like a wimp. Be nice: give a little "Hope all is well" icebreaker, and ask them what you wanted to ask.

When someone asks you for something, don't overdo it and give the person more than he or she asked for. Sure, when a boss asks for the Penske file, it certainly wouldn't hurt if you have the time to make sure it's all there, neatly organized in a manila folder. But when someone calls and asks for the phone number for Accounts Payable, don't offer to handle it yourself. The person wanted the phone number. Give him the phone number and move on.

The Vending Area

The vending area is like being on another planet. Sometimes it's replaced by the water cooler or the kitchen. Depending on your type of work space, you may have one, two, or all three of these areas. Similar to the bathroom, the vending area invokes a certain sense of camaraderie with fellow coworkers.

You might be two cubicles separated from someone in your office nine hours a day, but for the forty-five seconds you spend together while in the vending area, it's all fun, games, and Cheez-Its.

Sometimes the vending area can suck the good out of you. People say all the things they can't say around the office, even though the office is only about fifteen feet away. It becomes a place where coworkers conspire against both bosses and fellow coworkers. Be careful. A bigwig could be right around the corner.

Corporate Geography

Your work environment primarily depends on where you live. Whether it's the East Coast, West Coast, North Coast, or South Coast, everything from the wardrobe you wear to the types of coworkers you find are going to vary depending on your region. Certainly things will be different if you're working in Texas vs. working in Maine.

Don't be fooled, some areas ARE better to work in than others. It just depends on who you are and what you like. When you are ready to work, decide WHERE you want to work. Sometimes you have to decide where you want to live first; and then once you move there, you have to decide where you want to work. But remember, it's your life so YOU make the decisions.

You may prefer the fast pace that New York City offers. You may prefer an 8 a.m. to 7 p.m. workday. You may prefer your dinner to consist of either ordering a pizza to your cubicle or calling on your cell phone to Viang Ping during your walk home to have them deliver Pad Thai with chicken to your apartment in ten minutes. You may prefer long walks in the rain and snow to the stop-and-go freeways and metro and underground subway stations.

Phone pace in a big East Coast city like Boston or New York is significantly faster than the paces of those areas west and south. Talk to someone in Boca Raton or New Orleans and you'll see what I'm talking about. People from the South don't understand light-speed phone conversations. They like to start off every phone conversation with a "Hey, how are you doing there today?" And then the New Yorker or the Bostonian will just respond with "Fine." And then the southerner will still follow up with, "Well that's good to hear," and then preface whatever they are going to ask with another statement like, "Down here, we do service with a smile." After a quick comparison of their weather to your weather, you can finally get down to business.

If this same conversation took place between two New Yorkers, it would take fifteen seconds. It's all business. Big city workers don't put any toppings on their conversations. Get on the phone, find out what you need, get off the phone, move on. No smiles; no personal warmth. It's service with a stopwatch. Not that that's a good thing. Sometimes a little personality will go a long way. A lot of people are turned off by the coldness of a New York conversation. It's not natural but it does get the job done, so it's really just a matter of your personal taste.

Different geographies also have different types of food in the vending machine. Go look in a vending machine in the Midwest: Beef jerky, pork rinds, honey roasted peanuts, and Zagnut Bars. Go look at a vending machine in Los Angeles: 75 percent fat-free Sun Chips, bottled water, wheat pretzels, and soy protein bars. Check out a vending machine in New York City: Sugar, sugar, caffeine, sugar, and cough drops for the weekly sore throat.

While New Yorkers crave Snickers because they are constantly on the go, just the walk to work would be considered a marathon for people in the Midwest, who walk ten steps from their house to their car, spend twenty minutes in their car, and drive right up to their office. And both those areas are different from a city like Los Angeles, where you have to spend forty-five minutes on the 405 highway each morning just to go five miles. Cars breaking down, highways closed due to high-speed car chases (put down your cell phone and hurry home so you can watch it live from NBC 4's sky chopper!), smog indexes, and forest fires. If you're lucky, maybe you'll get an earthquake.

Know your geographic surroundings. Don't wear a Tommy Bahama shirt with a pair of Docksiders without socks if you're a bank teller in New Mexico. Save that for the folks in Miami, although oftentimes the temperature in your office will defy logic. If you live in a warm climate, your office will be FREEEEEZZZZINNNNGGG! Someone in your office will undoubtedly jack the air-conditioning to the low 60s. So if it's 80 degrees on average in your city, you may have to bring a sweater to work. On the other hand, if you live in a cold climate, your office will be SWELTERING. Someone in your office will have the temperature cranked up to 80. You could be in the midst of a long, cold Michigan winter, yet your office will feel like a tanning salon.

Cubicle design and overall office layout always varies from region to region. On the West Coast, you'll find that the entertainment industry and Internet offices are very modern, sleek, and artistically minded. Think, create, produce! In New York, space and efficiency are the two primary concerns. How can we fit seventy-five cubicles into a space that should only hold twenty-five? In any state that uses mountain standard time, space isn't at the same premium. You might have telemarketing or engineering companies that boast a more open atmosphere with cubicles that are less claustrophobic.

In the end there's only one office that will be to your liking: your office at home. The one place where you can sit in your underwear and tanktop, listen to downloaded music, and drink milk from the carton. Just don't confuse this with your company's "home office"; that could lead to problems.

Finally, if you have to travel frequently for your job, you have to react and adapt to ever-changing surroundings. Don't waltz into the local Cleveland sports bar and ask for a cosmo. If you're in town from Jackson Hole, don't walk into Spago in Beverly Hills and ask them if they've got Miller Lite on tap. Know your region and understand your surroundings.

Rigging the Office

The single most important thing you can do to ensure your longevity and improve your overall worth at the office is to rig it. I'm not talking about wiping your saliva on your bosses' phones if you hate them (they'll never know!) or putting a bucket of water on top of their doors. I mean refiling, reorganizing, and recomplicating things. Don't ever let your bosses know how to transfer calls, conference in calls, fix the computer, or find files. That's your job! And you can keep it as long as you spin a web of confusion thick enough to catch flies.

Think about it, if your bosses learns how to do all this, what do they need you for? As soon as you settle in and learn where everything is, change it. Put files in places that only you would know. Keep numbers and names away from the bosses and in special files on YOUR computer. They'll never know how to log on to your computer. Change passwords on both your and their computers. Simply tell them once that you've done this for "security reasons" and then never bring it up again. Tell them if they ever need it they should call you. This will probably only happen once a year, and they will have to call—making them realize how much they need you. That's a good thing.

Make it so your bosses can't do anything without you. Driving directions? Booking reservations? Ordering off Amazon? Expedia? What are the passwords?! Only you know! Fire you, get rid of you, and this will all be lost. You're invaluable until you decide it's time to move on.

Utilizing the Office

Remember in elementary school when you were hanging on the jungle gym during recess, and the bell would ring and some kids would just make a beeline for the school? Remember also how most of the time you wanted ten extra seconds on the swings? That's what utilizing the office should be like.

If you're not a boss, your sole reason for being there is to make money for the company. In return the company pays you less money than the amount you make for them. The more money they make, the more money you technically should make. But the fact is, salary alone will never land you happiness in the beginning. So while you're young, you need to do something else. Something more exciting than whatever it is you do for the company. With a little creativity, you can even run another business through your office.

The real way to utilize the office is to make it YOUR office. I knew a girl in Human Resources who ordered a background check on her boyfriend to see if he really used to play baseball for Florida State (he didn't). It doesn't matter what you do: freelance writing, cartooning, reading, editing, design, Web consulting, online opinions, DJ, counseling—do something! If you need to supplement your income, you've got the perfect place to do it. At every job I've ever worked, I've worked on three things. One is writing. That's when I wrote this book. I had the ability to write a page or so a day using their computer. Every day I had nine hours of access to their Internet (always cable or DSL, much faster than my dial-up at home) to research, print, copy, and download.

The second thing I did was work on a Web site. I didn't design one because I don't know how to do that, so instead I conceptualized one—and along with my friend and business partner (who lives by these same corporate rules) we built an online Web service from the ground up using the foundations of the companies we worked for as our home base. We used our computers to design business cards, color spreadsheets, marketing kits, flyers, labels, and stickers. When it was all said and done, we had a fully operational Web site built up.

Third, I produced a movie from work. Wrote it, directed it, and produced it. I had a friend design the graphics and logos, and I even printed a few $8^1/2 \times 11$ posters and press kits on the color printer. All of this was done carefully. I didn't go around bragging, and I didn't keep anything lying around the office.

Whatever you make or do, take it home or ship it out that day. You don't need someone going through your desk looking for the Penske file and stumbling upon a color press kit. To make a long story short, the movie made it into film festivals all over the country. I had an advantage that most indie filmmakers didn't have. I was backed by a corporation.

Don't steal things from work. It's not worth trying to steal stacks of paper or supplies. I mean if you want to throw a pen or a highlighter into your bag, fine. You should be able to, considering all the bullshit you have to put up with each day. The least they can do is let a highlighter slip by.

These are the three things that kept me sane through three years of working Corporate. I never understood how the several hundred or even thousands of people I worked with could just show up at work at 9 a.m., do their job, go home, stick their microwaved Healthy Choice meal into the microwave, watch *American Idol,* and be content with their lives, knowing that they had to get up the next day and do it all over again.

Maybe I do it all out of insecurity. Maybe I do it because I want to succeed, or I want money and the freedom it brings. I do know that the three things I do while at work I do because I love them. They keep me happy. That one person at your company who one day just ups and quits because they sold a book, a script, a Web site, or are partaking in a huge venture—be jealous. Because it could have been you.

Covering Your Tracks

Since you're at work you cannot always do as you please. Everything must be done on the fly, by the seat of your pants. And often times you can't, or don't, want the rest of the office to see what you are doing, know where you've been or what you've been up to. There are a few little tricks that could save you from an overly curious coworker:

MINIMIZE!

Suppose you want to check out the latest Lakers score on ESPN.com or order makeup from Sephora.com. If you do it at work, everyone will see you! Getting caught surfing the Internet is a no-win situation. If it's a boss who sees you, you've damaged your Promotion Potential. If it's a coworker, rest assured everyone will know.

So what to do? Minimize. When you see or hear someone coming your way, minimize the screen you are looking at on your computer. I've minimized three times in the last hour. Keep this screen as small as possible, and then also keep a decoy screen available. For instance, you may be looking at MTV.com, but behind it you should have the latest Penske Excel document up and running so when Barbara from Human Resources stops by to drop off a memo, you can quickly click in the top right corner of your screen, minimize your page, and all of a sudden . . . the Penske file is showing! It's like you've been working on it for hours, even though you now know the Lakers haven't scored in eight minutes!

CHANGING OF THE GUARD

At some point there will come a time when you're going to have to interview for another job. You aren't going to have the luxury of planning when the interview is. Sometimes, you've got a 1:30 p.m. interview scheduled during your lunch break. You can't wear your nice interview clothes without your coworkers noticing because they will casually joke, "Hey, going to an interview?" They know. Why? Because they've done it themselves.

Instead, bring a small bag to work and a change of clothes in it. Wear components. You could wear the pants or the skirt, but keep the top or jacket hidden and then change in the bathroom. Change from 1:00–1:05. Get in the car and you've got ten to fifteen minutes to get to the interview. Hopefully the interviewer won't be running late, and you'll have time to get back in your car, drive back to work, change back into your clothes in the bathroom, and be back at your desk pretending like Wendy's ninety-nine-cent value meal was the greatest thing that ever happened to you.

Pop Culture and the Office

Why isn't there anything good on the radio or the television anymore? Why don't more shows take risks? Television has become so bad I find myself watching CNN just to escape. The reason Britney Spears will have the #1 selling album in America is because most people buy it. That's simple math. But what isn't simple is that the people who bought the album are in your office, and they all think that Britney Spears is the best dancer with the greatest voice.

Listen to good music. Appreciate good movies. Don't rush to see the new Russell Crowe clichéd actioner the weekend it premieres. How many times can you see the same movie plot? Who cares if he finds the mob killers who took out his wife (don't worry, he will; and if he doesn't, you'll be paying to watch the even-more-predictable se-quel next summer). Go see the one with the subtitles that looks more interesting. You have to stimulate yourself outside of the office.

If you get sucked into the American culture of Coca-Cola and Disney, you are just another step toward losing yourself. Driving a Saturn because it's practical, shopping at the Gap during sales, and renting new releases at Blockbuster are all signs that you have grown up, matured, become practical, and now want to blend in with the clones. You will never rise to the top with this attitude. You might as well put down this book and go check your e-mail on America Online.

Don't get saturated in normalcy. You'll lose any edge you once had. Look at the bigwigs around the office. Do they wear clothes from the Gap? Do they drive a Saturn? It's all right there in front of you, so it's obvious what you should and should not do. You have to play the part of success if you want someone else to notice you. If you and Jim are equally qualified and both are up for a pro-motion in June, but you dress in slick, nicely dry-cleaned clothes that are really hip and snazzy, and you drive a sports car, a con-vertible, or an SUV—and he drives a Ford Taurus and dresses in Gap khakis with a blue button down and a white undershirt, who do you think is going to get the promotion?

It's sad to say, but it's true; and I've seen it happen countless times. And in the Corporate World, this is what matters. So when you wake up every morning, you have to decide, not just whether you are going to do a good job at work, but are you also going to do a good job at being Corporate? Every kid goes shopping a few days before starting their first job. You're going to blow a good $500 of your (or hopefully your parents') money on new digs for your new gig. No matter what your inner self is telling you, DO NOT SHOP AT THE GAP. Go somewhere with nice-looking clothes that will help you. There's no point in doing your job better than everyone else if you're going to dress exactly like them! It's like hitting the ball well but then not running to first base.

PART FOUR

THE RULES OF ENGAGEMENT

There are hundreds of unwritten rules and laws of the Corporate World. Most you'll pick up on quickly because they are common sense and necessary for your survival. Others are harder to apply. Here are some rules to live by that may or may not come naturally to you:

CHAPTER 7

ASK NOT WHAT YOUR COMPANY CAN DO FOR YOU

Business Cards and the Rolodex

HOW MANY TIMES HAVE YOU HEARD SOMEONE SAY, "It's all in who you know." Well, believe it or not, for once this advice is actually correct. Write down everyone's name after you meet them. Get their card. Doesn't matter if you give them yours, or if you even have one, although this is something you should ask for before you begin working. Business cards will help you build a network of people you will soon dislike, but it's an unfortunate mandate if you want to excel. The same people you wouldn't trust with your wallet are the ones who will come in handy later on.

It's sad that your job can boil your entire existence down to a couple of words on a 2×3-inch index card, and what's even sadder is that sometimes it may even take a good three years to get your first company business card. Fight for it if there's a possibility to get one. If you work for a small company, they'll usually give you cards because they need to use you to make contacts for them. If your company says they won't provide cards for you, but they'll allow you to get some if you pay for them yourself, do it. A business card enhances your stature tenfold. Most companies are too shortsighted to fit this small expenditure into their budget. But it's an extremely useful way to gather important information.

Always keep track of other people's information. If they give it to you, they want you to have it. So use it. You may meet someone who does security for the local arena. Call them when you need them. You may meet someone who works for a printing company. Call them when you need them. You may meet someone in publishing. Call them. Haven't spoken to them in two years? Doesn't matter. This is the beauty of e-mail. You can write them after two years and say, "Hey, I know we haven't spoken in a while—I hope all is well with you. Listen . . ."

Maybe they'll write back with a, "Hey!" or maybe they won't write back at all. Regardless, it's easier than a phone call. You can't do any of this, however, if you don't have their info in the first place. So keep a good Rolodex. Even if you speak to someone named Mary and you don't remember what she does or where she works or her last name or anything, write it down, put it under M in your Rolodex, and move on. You might need it one day.

Make sure no one else in your office has access to *your* Rolodex. It's yours, you've put in the work, and you should therefore only use it to benefit yourself. Don't share your contacts with coworkers; that's the equivalent of you doing their job. You're helping them excel. If you knew a coworker in high school, would you take the SATs for him or her? Of course not. Work is constantly a test, and every minute there's a new one. In the end, getting promoted is about how many tests you pass. Someone asking you for this kind of help is cheating. In college you can get expelled for this kind of shit.

Maybe you're an expert in a certain field and people come to you for certain names and numbers. That's fine if you're the expert. That's what you are—an expert in the field—so sure, share anything! No one can challenge you; no one can do a better job. But if they come to you and ask you for the name or number of that guy you were talking to at lunch last week, you may not want to let that info out. You then lose your competitive edge, which comes back to haunt you when Jim gets promoted ahead of you.

When you come into contact with bigwigs at other companies, put them in your Rolodex and make sure you get in theirs. Stay in touch with them at least once a year. Let's just say you have a random connection that somehow lands you a HUGE interview with a CEO of a major company. Now you might not have been ready for a job working for him; or the company might not have even had a job opening at that time—but you did in fact get to spend five minutes with him in his office during his busy day. Don't ever let that slip away.

Turn that five minutes into five years. One week after meeting with him, write a nice thank you. Just a quick little note with your address on the envelope in the return address slot. He'll have an assistant log your address into the Rolodex—and presto—you're in one of the most important Rolodexes in town. Now every year you can send him correspondence, something as simple as a quick e-mail, updating him on your stellar progress and wishing him a happy whatever (Christmas if it's December, Chanukah if he's Jewish, New Year if it's January). Soon you'll be ready to ask him for a job, and perhaps he may bring you in. The worst that could happen is he doesn't e-mail you back. And then you've lost nothing because you never really had anything with him in the first place.

The Handshake

For some reason it was decided centuries ago that two Americans cannot meet on a Corporate level unless one person extends their right hand and holds it against the palm of the other person. A simple exchange of germs meant to convey a personal greeting. Europeans air kiss, and the Japanese give cool little bows while the most powerful country in the world forms impressions through hand grips. If you catch a cold within your first week on the job, it's probably a good thing. It means you're meeting a lot of important people.

As you continue to assimilate, you will begin to meet more higher-ranking executives. And every one of them will want to place their palm against yours. You should want to give as many handshakes as you can, assuming you know what you're doing. It's fine to throw down a hip handshake with the mail guys when you see them, but with everyone else you want to make eye contact and establish a firm grip. You're shaking their hand and not vice versa. Handshakes are subtext, and this is your way to tell people that this is the business world and you mean business.

A bad handshake can ruin you. We're all familiar with the most common of the lame handshakes, "the dead fish," and we know it can do irreparable damage to your Promotion Potential. People subconsciously think that your handshake reveals what kind of worker you are. A weak handshake tells others that you are "timid" and "insecure," not the type of aggressive person looking to excel.

Then there's the clammy handshake. If you sense your hands are clammy DO NOT SHAKE HANDS WITH ANYONE. If you shake someone's hand and afterward they have to wipe their hands on their pants, that's something they'll always remember. They'll probably tell other people about it, and then you'll get a stigma attached to you.

Luckily, for the times when you're caught off guard and you fear you're about to slime someone, there're many different stalling techniques you can employ to get you out of the handshake obligation. You can try the universal head nod, or you can give a military salute. Believe it or not, even a Fonzie-style, "Aaaaaaay!" will make you look cooler than a handshake that originated from below sea level.

Sometimes you'll go to shake someone's hand—the eye contact is perfect, the hand size is equal—but for some reason you both flail at the hand-gripping part. You accidentally just squeeze the person's fingers or she overextends her hand and suddenly she's grabbing your wrist. Don't worry, these are mutually understood failed handshakes. You'll make embarrassed eye contact with the other person as you pull away, but you both know it's not your fault and you both know that no one else is going to know about it. It's a flaw in the system, about one in every hundred handshakes will not connect.

The Hours

Five days on, two days off . . . for the next thirty years. And what makes matters worse is that the days of working the typical nine to five are long gone. If you took any sociology classes in college, you know that in most cases, nine to five has turned into nine to six. In some places it's nine to seven. But whatever it is to you, rest assured, it's not accurate. That's because if you really want to break down your work hours, you'd have to include all of the hours that are part of your work week that you don't get paid for.

If you've got to be at work at 9:00, you most likely need to leave your house by at least 8:40. So that's twenty minutes right there that you had to spend for work purposes that you don't get paid for. And if you really wanted to push it, technically you have to get up at 7:40—you spend another hour to shit, shower, and primp yourself. And when you're at work you can't leave at exactly 5:00 p.m., it will make you look like a clock watcher. So maybe you stay until 5:10 p.m. That's 50 minutes a week! The 50 minutes a week you spend not being a clock watcher and the 20 minutes a day you spend getting to work and then the 20 minutes you spent getting home is 250 minutes a week! That's over 4 hours a week! That's 208 hours a year! And you don't get paid for any of it.

Expect to work your ass off when you first get hired. In a perverse way, you may actually want to. You may find yourself working extra hard, going that extra mile to show your superiors that they made the right choice when they hired you. But that initial feeling is fleeting, and soon you'll know the location of every clock on your floor. That is, if they've given you clocks, but let's assume for the moment you're not making Nikes in Southeast Asia.

Your real office hours will be different from what they told you during your meeting with Barbara in Human Resources. After a two-week grace period, you'll get a feel for what the real hours will be. Once you see how many hours your coworkers put in, it's once again vital that you find that happy medium.

Don't become a *Late Stayer*. These are the people who at, let's say, 6 p.m. or 7 p.m., when you are supposed to leave, stay at work and hang out. Usually they talk on the phone and make their long-distance calls (I commend those people). Others just simply have no life.

If you really think about it, work *is* your life. Other than sleeping, you probably will only spend about three to four hours a day at home. Compare that with the eight to ten hours you'll spend at work, and you'll see why the Late Stayers have their priorities mixed up.

The important lesson to learn here is when to arrive and when to leave. Your arrival is the most important part of the day because it sets the tone for the day ahead. In the morning you don't want to arrive late and have to walk past everyone already at their desk. You undoubtedly will be the recipient of all sorts of comments, "Late night last night?" "Couldn't get up this morning?" "Traffic?" Fact is, occasionally those WILL be the reasons. But usually it's just that you were running late and it's not anyone else's business. So don't run late. If you have to be at work at 9:00, you need to plan your morning routine around being at work at 8:55.

Although this is only five minutes early, it can make or break your day. It will give you time to get settled and get breakfast, if you so desire. It will give you time to check your voice mail and e-mail without other people in the office around to distract you. It will allow you to sit at your desk for five minutes without having to answer the phone if it rings . . . because technically you're not supposed to be there yet.

You'll be at your desk with your head down with the appearance of already working when everyone else is just arriving. You know the old saying, "The early bird gets the worm." People will see you there early, and it sends a message. They know you work hard and "hardworking" is an adjective you want used to describe you. Especially by your boss. You always want to beat your boss to work.

In terms of leaving, however, it's just the opposite. First, you can't leave until after your boss leaves. It sucks, but unfortunately you don't get to leave until they do. After they leave, you still don't want to be the first of your peers to leave. On the other hand, you also don't want to be the last person to leave either. It's bad for your Corporate Identity, especially if you are seen by others on their way out. You don't want to be the last person there when even the Late Stayers have given up and the cleaning crew is vacuuming.

Leaving time is the time when you want to blend in. Leave just after everyone else leaves. Sure, leaving with everyone else signifies that you can leave whenever you want, a personal freedom, but leaving two minutes after the main crowd makes it looks like you've got some quick stuff to finish. You'll be leaving soon, just not "now." It also signifies that you want to finish your work for the day.

You don't want to hang back too long though. Staying there too long makes it look like you can't do all your work in one day. It could mean you're incompetent; it could mean you're overwhelmed; or it could mean you're slow. It could also mean you are a hard-worker, but you could still be a hardworker and leave earlier.

Last, don't give the illusion that you've left early. Nothing gives off that illusion more than a turned-off computer, a pushed-in chair, and a neat desk. People will walk by your area and they'll know you're gone. So leave your computer on, maybe even keep a program open on your computer. If they see your chair is not pushed into your desk, if maybe your pens and paper are still out, they might think to themselves, "Hey, did Jim in Marketing leave?" And they'll ponder it and move on. What they won't know is whether you left or not. Maybe even keep an extra sweater or jacket to throw on the back of your chair. Your coworkers will think you just went out to grab a bite or are around the corner in the bathroom.

Taking a Lunch

Lunchtime is sacred time. The phones won't ring as much, the Power Lunch bosses are all out chowing on surf and turf, and a sense of peace generally reigns supreme. If you're just starting out and you need to make an impression, sometimes you may have to work through lunch. But if you have no work obligations, get outta there!

The sense of peace is nice and all, but if that's all you want, go work at a campground. It doesn't matter if you have Ariel Sharon and Yassir Arafat on a conference call, when it's time to take a lunch, hang up and go get yourself some fresh air. Use lunch to get away from the structured chaos of your office. Don't sit at your desk like you do the rest of the day. You wouldn't sit there if you didn't have to, and your lunch break is the only time when you don't have to.

Every once in a while, however, you will have to eat lunch at your desk. That's fine, just beware of the *Lunch Peekers*. These people are the main reason I hate to eat lunch at my desk. Lunch Peekers are the in-laws of the Corporate World. They'll drop by your cubicle when you least expect it. You'll be sitting there, enjoying a nice, hot chicken parmesan, and all of a sudden you see a head slowly rise over the cubicle divider. "Hey buddy, how was your weekend, whaddya think about that memo from Accounts Receivable?"

It goes from bad to worse when the Lunch Peekers see you have food at your desk. They will peek into your cubicle or over your desk and stare down at your food, "Mmm, whatcha got there? Looks good." Or "Ugh, what is that smell?" Lunch Peekers tend to be more critical when you're eating something hot that has a strong odor, too. Can you believe that? Leave us alone! Let us eat in peace!

If you become the "go-to" guy for something, you'll get "gone-to" even during your lunch break. If you happen to be eating lunch at your desk, you will get disturbed. The longer you work there, the more people will come to trust and depend on you. Some coworkers just don't believe in the sacredness of taking a lunch.

Obviously, sitting in a rickety chair at a narrow desk staring at a computer isn't going to give you a six-pack and strong thighs. It's only going to cause you to drink a six-pack and order three pieces of thighs from KFC. And since you're not a spring chicken anymore, you'll have to eat healthier than you used to. Your metabolism is slowing down and everything you eat is going to add inches to your waistline. As a kid, you eat a slice of pizza and it passes right through you. It just makes you grow taller. Eat a slice of pizza now, and it makes you grow wider.

So eat quality food when you can. Compensate for the days when you're forced to eat Chinese food at your desk. Get out and eat a healthy meal with vegetables and foods that aren't high in fat, cream, butter, or cholesterol. Motherly advice no doubt, but in the grand scheme of things, the better you eat the better you will feel. And the better you feel, the better you will act at work.

Remember that everything you do is scrutinized under a giant microscope. Everyone is watching you all the time so you have to be careful about what you eat and how you eat it. That's why it's so important to NOT PACK YOUR OWN LUNCH. People are watching. Take a quick look at those people at your office who pack their own lunch. Look at the introverted little pack of drones who always eat lunch together. Are any of them successful? Hell no! They're probably just a bunch of Late Stayers! Do the bosses pack their own lunch? Of course not.

Packing your own lunch shows a weakness. It shows "home." It shows "save money." Those aren't characteristics you want at work if you are trying to enhance your Promotion Potential. If you have to pack your own lunch, at least don't let anyone see it. Keep it in your car. At least while you're chowing on chicken salad in the underground parking lot, no one else knows it so at least you're giving the illusion that you're an important person who has to take a lunch. Eating out shows them you can do whatever you want. It shows them you're not the fifty-five year old on the special fiber diet.

When all else fails and you can't eat out, at least make sure you bring in something from the outside world. Delivery is nice because, for a few seconds, it let's you feel like someone else is catering to you. But regardless, always have food from the outside world. Think of the extra $6 a day as an investment. You're sending a message to your coworkers who don't know your salary. "Hey, I can afford to eat out for lunch. Five times a week." It's no different than showering, dressing nicely, and doing your job right.

It's all part of the image you're pretending to portray in order to increase your Promotion Potential.

That said, there is one huge drawback if you leave your desk for lunch: Getting People Food. Numerous times throughout the day, a coworker will say, "I'm going out for coffee, does anyone want anything?" and usually everyone's like, "No thanks, I'm good." Until it's YOUR turn. And since you've seen that it's common courtesy to ask others if they want anything when you make a food run, now you have to ask too. So you say, "I'm going out, does anyone want anything?"

And of course, some annoying jerk will be like, "Oohhh, I could really go for an apple danish and coffee." And then he'll give you money and say, "I'll take a few packets of Equal and a side of cream, too. And if they don't have apple danish get me cheese danish, anything but blueberry." Of course that will make other people hungry and all of a sudden you've got to break out the Post-it pad and write all of this down. All you wanted was a bagel and now you're a waiter. Be prepared to get a $20 bill for each $1.50 order. Nobody will ever have correct change.

You already have to work all day, you don't want to work when you're just getting yourself some food. But essentially that's what you're doing; working more. If someone gives you an order for food, that's work. They've just given you work. You're now catering to someone else, and you don't even get a tip! The worst part is when you get home later, you'll still have a little yellow sticky note in your pocket as a harsh reminder. It's all in a day's work; but hey, at least you made it home.

The Bored Meeting

Not to be confused with the Board Meeting, that's when the VPs get together in a valiant attempt to impress the bigwigs who would just as soon fire them to save a nickel a share. Some places call it the Monday morning status meeting. Some places call it the creative meeting or the development meeting. Whatever it's called— it's grandstanding at its best, and your company is bound to have them on occasion.

When a meeting is called, rest assured only 10 percent of the people in the meeting actually want to be there. The person leading the meeting wants to be there. Why wouldn't they; that person gets to run the damn thing. The goodie-goodie wants to be there; this is his or her chance to speak out and say something they deem meaningful. The people who like to hear themselves talk want to be there, too. You know them—the ones who preface everything with, "I think . . ."—as if you care. Everyone else in the room is just meditating with their eyes open, partially absorbing what is being said.

I don't really mind meetings. I actually find them quite productive. I keep my mouth shut most of the time and work on my errand or grocery list. Use meetings to think about all the people you need to call back, plan for the weekend, or figure out a clever way to get out of jury duty. The irony is that sometimes it's hard to stay focused on the things that really matter. Don't get distracted by the girl with the lazy eye or the guy with the weird wart thing on his neck.

Oftentimes in meetings, you do actually feel the need to voice your opinion. When you speak up, make sure you're saying something worthwhile and that the timing is right. If you make one statement over the course of three bored meetings, say it right and it could have more of an effect than those who run their mouth twenty times every meeting. That's also the beauty of intelligence. You tend to already know and have a plan vs. the person who is not intelligent and thinks everything is a genius idea.

The most important thing to remember in bored meetings is how to deal with conflict. Is the point of whatever you are going to say to disagree with whatever was just said or do you really believe in your idea? If you really believe in your idea, say it in a manner to not necessarily disagree with whatever was just said. For instance, Jim in Marketing might say, "I think our new corporate logo should include the color blue." Rather than just coming out and saying, "I don't think so; I think we should consider purple," you should phrase it something like, "I think Jim's got a good point. We should check into this further. I was reading about the psychology of colors and I found that purple actually exudes leadership and royalty, and since we . . ." and that way you've kind of made nice on both sides and you've given off a positive vibe to the whole situation. Some people are just negative by nature, and they give off negative vibes to the tune of negative statements. Don't be that person.

CHAPTER 8

CORPORATE DO'S AND DON'TS

Smoking, Booze, and Drugs

DEPENDING ON WHERE YOU WORK AND FOR WHOM you work, these can be no-no's or yes-yes's. Smoking cigarettes is a new stigma that you may not want branded on you. It's best to not let your bosses know you smoke cigarettes because smoking kills you. You already know that. So if your bosses know you inhale something all day that kills you, what are they going to think about you? Unless they smoke, too. Then puff away, and bring them a carton for their birthday. Cancer for everyone!

Now with the booze, be sure to at least partake every once in a while. I've seen studies that say moderate drinkers actually earn more than abstainers. Don't be the straight edge who never touches the stuff, but most importantly, never be the resident alcoholic who shows up hungover every morning. Make sure your bosses know you enjoy a tall, cold one every now and then. Find out what kind of booze they like and buy them a bottle for their birthday.

As for drugs, go with the Nancy Reagan viewpoint of, "Just Say No." On all accounts, say no. Say no to weed and coke and pain killers and muscle relaxers and Xanax. They're going to be all over the office. Every secretary will have pain killers and muscle relaxers, all of the mail room guys will have weed, the male execs will have the coke, and the females will have the Valium, Xanax, and Ativan. Stay away from all of it when it's offered it to you.

If you have your own, fine. Keep it at home. But at work, you don't need Mary in research to give you a pill and then tell Jane she gave you one. Don't smoke pot after the Christmas party with your fellow employees. Of course it's cool to make jokes about it. You can even let people in on any stories you may have from your college days, but don't ever do anything with any of these people. They are your workmates; never confuse them with friends.

Sexual Harrassment Policies

Seems like everyone in America is waiting for a settlement. Whether it's fat kids suing McDonald's or a drunken fan who got his ass kicked for running on the baseball field, everyone is looking for a way to cheat the system. Filing a frivolous lawsuit has become the easy way out. And not only is it easy, but people unhappy or dissatisfied with their jobs see it as the easiest way to end Corporate Life.

It seems almost too easy to "earn" a huge settlement. And if you can't find your way to the Neverland Ranch for a piece of Michael Jackson, why not target the sex drive of your fellow coworkers? What easier way to make money than to target the most dominant impulse in the human body? Sexual suits are so common in America you can practically buy them at JCPenney's. Everyone from Clarence Thomas to Thomas Jefferson could sport their own line.

Let's be honest. If you're a twenty-two-year-old guy and you're in good shape and you take care of yourself, dress well, and groom well—whom do you think the single, thirty-five-year-old female VP is going to want to have sex with? You or the forty-six-year-old father of three, head of research with a gut the size of the box of donuts he ate this morning? And if you are a twenty-two-year-old woman, strutting around in your new heels and Bebe outfit, whom do you think EVERY guy in the office is going to want to get with? You or the pregnant woman sitting in her cubicle eating mashed potatoes with ketchup on top? Weird fetishes aside, people are going to want to sleep with you, so it's best to understand what's going on.

Any job in the Corporate World will come with Sexual Harassment rules and regulations restricting the very impulses that control our lives. And since your company hopes to avoid lawsuits, they will be as ambiguous as possible with the language, leaving doubt as to where the line in the sand is actually drawn between flirting and indecency.

Of course they'll tell you that Sexual Harassment is prohibited by the company and is against the law, but no one ever reads the brochure and everyone has their own definition of what sexual harassment is. At most companies they'll tell you it's forbidden to ask a coworker out on a date. The reason is that the basis for a Sexual Harassment claim is always determined by the other party. What one may deem proper may be severely improper to another—hence, the company is not chancing anything. Sterile, sex-free, nonconfrontational, "Hello, thank you, see you later," situations.

It's the most important policy in the office, yet it's completely subjective and only reinforces just how cold and sterile the office really is. Pretty much anywhere else in the world you can walk up to people and tell them how beautiful they are. They might get a little freaked out depending on the situation or the location, but assuming you're not a pedophile, it's a flattering compliment. Now imagine you're in the office, someone brings you the Penske file, and you say, "Thanks. You are really beautiful." If ever there was a moment where a record player scratched, time came to a screeching halt, and people stared at you like your fly was down, it's now.

I'm not saying you have to walk around the office like Charlie Puritan. But before you go around quoting your best lines from the Bill Clinton Almanac, feel out your office and see what your coworkers are like. See if the Maternity Mom is cool before you make any jokes about dating her newborn. If you see the nature-loving secretary put something in the recycling bin, don't show her a box of condoms about to expire and ask her if she believes in wasting things. There's always a fine line and sometimes even that line has exceptions. Don't tell any of your favorite jokes until after you've been there for a couple of weeks and only when you're in the bathroom, then it's okay. Don't pinch unless it's St. Patrick's Day, then it's okay.

I've never witnessed Sexual Harassment firsthand. It seems like the most exclusive country club in the world, only there's no golf. Sexual Harassment happens behind closed doors, and I never seem to be on the right side of the door. The only thing I really know is that it never happens how you'd imagine. In the movies it's depicted with horrible clichés about the old executive and the cute newbie, innocent enough to do anything for a promotion. The executive makes a proposition and says something like, "If you do this for me, I'll make sure it's worth your while." This isn't how it goes down in real life though. Bigwigs don't walk around the halls making overt propositions to members of the opposite sex. They don't spank you on the ass if you miss the morning meeting. It's more subtle than that, and this kind of "advancement" is wrong no matter how you look at it.

Fishing Off the Company Pier

This is a real can of worms.

Interoffice dating works for some people and chances are high that if you're at your job long enough, two people you work with may tie the knot. During my first summer internship in California, our receptionist was dating one of the junior executives. Toward the end of my internship, they got engaged. She told me it was the biggest decision of her life; she'd made a decision to spend every waking moment of her life with another human. It's a crazy decision to have to make, and a decision I didn't appreciate at the time. I was standing there in my studio apartment, trying to decide if the brown spot on the edge of my pepper jack cheese was mold or a bread crumb. Back then, those were the big decisions I faced in my life.

A week after their engagement was announced, I was praying for my internship to end. All day long the receptionist sat at her chair, looking at wedding catalogues and asking me for advice, as if I'd been married a million times. Her entire focus shifted; and since I was just the lowly intern, I kept hearing about all her wedding problems. I noticed that most of them concerned her coworkers. Should she invite the whole office? Should she only invite her little lunch clique? Maybe she should just invite her floor but no one else?

Office weddings have their pros and cons. They have pros because, hey—free wedding! Cake, ice cream, dancing, booze, single bridesmaids, single groomsmen—and you don't have to worry about anything. But the con is that you have to go—why the hell would you want to go to a wedding with people from work?

Although it worked out for the receptionist, I've heard enough office romance war stories to fill a Civil War museum. I therefore have to argue that generally speaking, dating someone in your office isn't worth the awkwardness.

As usual, I think the media is partly to blame for the way office romance is glamorized. On TV, they make interoffice dating full of wonder and excitement. Remember all those times on *Melrose Place* when Heather Locklear got a newbie alone in her office? Within seconds, everything on the desk is flying off onto the floor and they're passionately making out. It was sexy office romance, and it had our entire country imagining what it would be like to be a part of the Office Folklore. But is it worth becoming an urban legend among your coworkers?

Assuming you won't mind becoming instant gossip fodder, there are still several unsavory situations you'll encounter that they don't show on TV. Let's say you go out with the office knockout one night, hit it off, and the next thing you know, she's in your bedroom wearing your button down on the way to the bathroom. Sure it's the sexiest thing you've ever seen at that present moment, but what about the next day. What do you do?

Obviously, you have options. You both can flaunt the new relationship, let everyone know, be confident, and see what happens. This is great at first, but what if things don't work out? You can't keep doing this, you'll build a reputation, and after a while, someone's gonna complain to Human Resources (unless you work in the restaurant industry).

You can try to go the concealment route and not let anyone know about your budding new relationship. But then you will have to sketch around the office all day, worrying about looking at each other too long, wondering what other people will say. You'll end up avoiding the very person you want to see the most. This will only compound your already complicated work experience. Don't make things even harder on yourself.

The *Wall Street Journal* recently ran a story saying that office romance is on the rise. Ever wonder why divorce rates are, too?

Gossip

Like colds in a kindergarten class, gossip is everywhere. It's on every phone, every computer, in every mouth. It's everywhere. You need to participate, but at what level? People will gossip about personal lives. They'll gossip about salaries, vacation, sex, promotions, you name it. Keep abreast of all the gossip; after all, it's gossip! It's good to know and it's fun!

Coworkers will always gossip; they just can't help themselves. And if they don't have anything legitimate to gossip about, they'll invent something. Gossipers literally come in all shapes and sizes. Some enjoy dishing it out; some prefer to sponge it up. While many only focus on "the big stories," others simply have to know everything that's going on. They build up stockpiles of useless information that has nothing to do with them. There will be others still who are always at your desk in the mornings waiting to greet you with, "Hey, did you hear about so and so?" They spend the entire day floating from cubicle to cubicle gathering juicy gossip. If only they were as diligent at their job as they are in spreading rumors. In exchange for sharing their inane news with you, they will expect some nugget of information in return—and that's when you have to be careful.

Don't be the one spreading rumors, and don't gossip on a proactive level, especially when you sense that things are getting downright nasty. Fact is, backstabbing is alive and well in the Corporate World. Sure, those people will be talking smack about someone at 2:22 p.m., but I guarantee you that by 3:15 p.m. they'll all be having coffee together—with the person they were talking about! And guess what they'll be doing? Talking about someone else! It's all reminiscent of the gossipy cliques of high school—the difference is now they've had twenty extra years of practice!

Participate in the gossip game with your boss. Discreetly keeping your boss apprised of some of the more pertinent gossip will win you points, big time! Bosses like to feel included, from a distance of course, and they may even pass along some of the juiciest gossip from the top echelon that you'd otherwise not be privy to.

When to Speak Out Against Your Boss

On many occasions, especially in meetings, your boss will ask for your opinion. Or rather, they will ask for your opinion, which is really supposed to be just their opinion restated in your high-pitched nasally business voice. The subtext of these moments is that you have to automatically reflect whatever they're saying. If afterward you want to disagree—do so privately. Say something like, "Listen, I said that I agreed with you . . . but really I think it might be best if . . ."

This advice, however, must come with a disclaimer because some bosses may respond to that with, "Why are you wasting my time telling me something first, then telling me something completely different now?" Other bosses may never want to hear your second "private" opinion. I worked with a VP once who'd gotten an amazing job offer to work for a rival company. The only drawback was that his new boss had one of the worst reputations in the entire industry. The VP thought that this new boss couldn't be as bad as everyone was saying, so he took the offer. Six months after he took the job, he sat down with her and told her he didn't like the way she was treating a few of the other employees. She said that she appreciated his opinion, then gave him till the end of the day to clear out his office.

Whether the opinion is creative or business could also affect whether you should speak up. If it's a creative opinion they want, you may want to give it to them. After all, if you were hired for your creativity, then you should have some sort of knowledge or input for the task at hand. Therefore, you should lend your young, hip, MTV ideas to the discussion. But if it's business, most of the time it's best to agree with whatever miscalculated half thought your boss has floated out into the Corporate ether. Part of increasing your Promotion Potential is figuring out which type of bosses you have and recognizing whether or not they care what you think.

It's good to care. Caring is good. Really. But guess what? Chances are your company won't care. There's an agenda for everything, and 99 percent of the time you'll find that things are the way they are for a reason. So if you have a suggestion on how to make things better, most of the time you should keep it to yourself. Because, technically speaking, in the eyes of upper management, a suggestion is merely a complaint. "I have a new way to get more bang for our buck" means all day you think the company is wasting money. Don't suggest it. You're not going to see any of that money reflected in your paycheck, so don't bother suggesting it.

Most of the time, suggesting something, like a way to make things run more efficiently, is going to require you to write a memo or have a quick meeting with management. You don't want to accrue too many of these meetings because you're going to need at least one or two of these for personal reasons when you really need more time off because your uncle is having surgery or you want a raise because you feel you are an invaluable member to the team. So don't add another meeting to your slate just so you can say, "I don't think the production team is moving as quickly as possible." Of course, know that if it's a huge idea it could lead to a promotion. A genius idea is the best way to get to the top. Just make sure your idea is genius, and sit on it for a while. Don't just spit it out forty-five minutes after you think of it.

Most importantly, never speak out if you think that something isn't "fair." In school, when something isn't "fair" you go and talk to an advisor, counselor, or teacher. Not the case in the Corporate World. If something isn't fair, you suck it up. You can't be a whistle blower. Don't be Erin Brockovich.

Sure it's not fair that in certain jobs, the harder you work, the less you get paid. But that's just the way it is. You should not complain to your boss that Jim in Marketing doesn't work as hard as you do, or leaves early all the time, or spends half of his day instant messaging his buddies, and that it's unfair he makes more than you do. First of all, you don't know Jim's situation. He could be the boss's second-cousin-once removed through marriage. Secondly, it makes you look like a whiner. Anyway, you need Jim. He makes you look good. If Jim didn't suck so bad, you might not look like the champion you are.

CHAPTER 9

OFFICE ETIQUETTE

Voice Mail Etiquette

*EVERY CORPORATE VOICE MAIL STATES THE OB-*vious; the person is either on the phone or away from their desk. No one is going to tell you that they're sitting right there but just don't feel like answering the phone right now. But this happens all the time. Half the voice mails you get are because you didn't want to pick up the phone. You sat there and let it ring so you didn't have to talk to anyone. But that's fine. You wouldn't want them to pick up the phone if you were calling them either. That would mean you'd actually have to talk to them.

View voice mail as an exchange of information. It's like you're talking to the person, only they're not there to interrupt and ask annoying questions. Say whatever you need to say and move on to a more important order of business, like what you're ordering for lunch.

There's nothing more annoying than a voice mail that doesn't actually tell you anything; it only sets you up for the ambush. Incorrect voice mail message: "Hi, this is Barbara, gimme a call when you have a second to discuss something." This will only annoy the person who was either on the other line or away from his or her desk. When you call back, you'll be ill-prepared because you won't know what the other person wants to discuss. Barbara will have the upper hand, and you have the disadvantage. Correct voice mail message: "Hi, this is Barbara, I'm calling about the proposal. I think we need to rework Section A and the conclusion." Now you can make sure you have that part in front of you when you return the call and maybe now you also have a couple of ideas of your own about how to improve Section A. Of course, if you're the one leaving the voice mail, none of this applies. Be as general as possible in order to maintain the upper hand.

Cell Phone Etiquette

Cell phones have become a necessary extension of the office. In fact your cell phone voice mail could be your most important tool. As widely as cell phones are used these days, there ought to be some sort of etiquette the world should adhere to. So allow me.

Don't you hate it when you get off of a plane, or wake up in the morning, and there are six rambling messages waiting for you? Keep it simple when leaving cell phone messages. Listen for the tone, leave your name, give your number, say what you have to say, state your number again, and then hang up. Keep your message under twenty seconds. Don't spend another thirty seconds afterward saying, "So if you get a chance, give me a call, or if not I'll call you; but either way let's catch up sometime soon. Hope all is well and I'll talk to you soon. Alright, take care." Just say, "Bye." I've got five other messages to listen to.

These days everyone has a cell phone, and everyone gets calls while they are at work. Some of your coworkers will answer their phone every time it rings; others recognize that this is not the most intelligent thing to do. Some people keep their phone on the loudest possible ringer, then they sit there and chat it up for hours. This behavior will piss off everyone at the office. Everyone else is doing their work, and this obnoxious coworker is talking to an old friend he just found on Google. Not to mention he has Kool & the Gang as his selected ring tone, which makes you even more bitter because you have nothing to "celebrate." It is best just to keep your phone on vibrate; and when you get a call you want to answer, you can politely excuse yourself, sprint down the hall, and handle your business privately.

Losing My Religion

No matter what series of outdated superstitions you subscribe to, Religion will always be the biggest taboo in the office. Yet if you really break it down, Religion is the perfect metaphor for Corporate Life: everyone's got an opinion, but no one knows the right answer.

In college it was cool to talk about Religion. You talked about it when you wanted to, and you didn't have to go to churches or temples unless you felt like it. Atheism was on the rise like never before, and you were exposed to some interesting theories about creation (sorry all you Agnostics—didn't want to leave you out). Make sure you get it all out of your system before you graduate, however, because it's definitely not kosher to walk around the office waxing poetic about the New Testament.

Arguing is fine and, in some cases, it's even encouraged. But religious arguments aren't the type of arguments you want to have in the Corporate World. People in the office are generally older, they've been around longer, they've heard it all before, and chances are they're set in their ways. They don't need the newbie talking to them about spirituality. Even if you were the Second Coming, chances are they'd ignore you.

There's nothing wrong with religious types floating around your office, but they are usually the ones who get offended the easiest. If you want to find the religious individuals, take a moment to notice who takes the time to display a religious ornament on or around his or her desk. Look for a crucifix, a menorah, or that Darwin fish-looking thing.

Don't be surprised to find some of the more abstract religions at the office. I used to work with some Jehovah's Witnesses. I found it amusing how they don't believe in any holidays, yet when it was time for their Christmas bonus, they were the first ones knocking on the door.

The best thing about Religion is that it gives you a couple of days off from Corporate Life. I'm surprised more executives don't convert to Judaism, especially when the High Holy Days roll around.

Seeing Coworkers in Public

It's going to happen. It's inevitable. Think of how many people are in your office. Fifty? Seventy-five? Two hundred? Odds are you are going to see them outside of the office, somewhere, sometime. The movies, Giovanni's Italian Bistro, or maybe even the gym. Say hi if it's applicable, meaning, if it's someone higher up on the totem pole. You don't want to look like you're avoiding them. It's even better if they have someone with them because it makes them look good and it's yet another contact you will make.

Certain times, however, you have to use caution. For instance, Jim in Marketing claims he has a girlfriend, but you see him close-talking to a very effeminate-looking man at a bar—steer clear of that. No need to put him in an uncomfortable position. Or you may see Barbara from Human Resources sitting by herself, reading the paper in a Starbucks. She could be a loner but doesn't want you to know that—so steer clear of her, too. But everyone else, give 'em a quick, "What's up," and move on. It's a positive encounter that for the most part makes you look like a pretty normal guy with a good life.

Listening to Music

Music illustrates the disparity between our generation and that of our parents. You can accurately compare the work ethic of a newbie with that of an older adult just by looking at the names of the bands that both generations grew up with. We had bands with nice soft syllable names like Everclear and Nirvana. They had bands like Earth, Wind & Fire and Blood, Sweat, and Tears, hard names that are indicative of natural disaster and toil. They smell blood and sweat while we smell teen spirit. Bob Dylan sang, "A Hard Rain's A-Gonna Fall," while his nice little son gave us the "Wallflowers." Weeeeeeee!

We'd all like to listen to music while at work, if only for the slight notion that it removes some of the work stigma and the stench of accountability. But this really depends on your type of work. Chances are that if your shoes match your belt, music is discouraged at the workplace. It's unlikely that anyone on the top floor of Morgan Stanley is listening to the Ramones on their CD-ROM. But if you can untuck your shirt at work, it's probably more of a laid-back atmosphere. Music may be allowed.

Listening to music at work is the ultimate way to keep yourself happy, if you can pull it off. It's a sad day when your office puts restrictions on music. That's when you realize how "unfree" you really are during the day. Sometimes on a Friday, a power-outage, an earthquake, snow, thunderstorm, or a partially observed holiday, you can play a CD on your computer at a barely audible level.

And it's not your favorite CD; it's just whatever was in your office, or whatever anyone else happened to have in their Discman at the bottom of their gym duffel bag. But you couldn't care less what it is—it's music. It's stimulating and, like music should always be, playing it at work is rebellious. And that's music to my ears.

I don't want to sound like too much of a loser, but working a Corporate job forces you to turn the music down. Unfortunately, you're surrounded by people older and less hip than you. As much as you want to fly into the parking lot blasting your Kenwood, it's not going to get you promoted. Turn your music down before you get in there. The last thing you need is for one of your bosses to drive up in a BMW 745i and see you banging on your dashboard, wearing Oakleys, rapping about "sippin on gin and juice."

On that same note, for all of you city folk who take mass transit to work—take your headphones off before you enter the building. Odds are you've got the volume turned all the way up on your gigantic headphones connected to your fluorescent orange CD player. Again, you don't need to get on the elevator with one of your bosses who is wearing her $1,000 Gucci outfits while Rage Against the Machine is screaming, "I'm Rolling down Rodeo with a shotgun . . ." It definitely lowers your Promotion Potential.

Grace Periods

These are unspoken, commonly understood spaces of time, usually on Fridays after 5 p.m. and on Mondays before 10 a.m., when nothing important gets done. Morning grace periods are subjective, and sometimes they're even ignored by the "morning people." I'm not one of these people, so as a general rule I never answer the phone before 10 a.m. on a Monday "mourning." Nothing is worth stressing over during the worst hour of the week. On Friday afternoons I like to start winding down a couple of hours after lunch. By then I've received some e-mails announcing weekend parties, and my mind begins to wander.

Grace periods also exist in the hours leading up to a federal holiday. The day before President's Day, Labor Day, July Fourth, etc., the grace period scale slides back a couple of hours. Your bosses may even give you a half day. But not everyone has generous bosses interested in preserving company morale. That's why you'll have some people who will call you at 5:45 p.m. on the Friday before July Fourth, looking for answers to some unimportant question that could easily have waited until the following week. The last thing I want to do is think about work (unless you count fire*works*).

The most obvious grace period that should be observed by everyone in Corporate America is the day before your company closes for Christmas. With so much love and good spirit in the air, nothing really gets done. There's so much food in the kitchen you need a whole day just to sample all the offerings. A coworker with a gourmet spouse will bring in a pound cake, and a client will send over a brownie platter that's richer than your boss. Enjoy this day. Eat enough brownies to turn yourself into a fat cat. If you have that semi-important report to write up, ask yourself if it can wait until after the New Year. No one's gonna read it anyway.

PART FIVE

TOO MANY FREAKS, NOT
ENOUGH SHOWS

There are two types of people in the world: those who say there are two types of people in the world, and those who know better. In order to get promoted, you must know and understand your coworkers. Get a feel for their many strengths and weaknesses.

While there are many different variations of coworkers you will meet throughout your corporate tenure, several distinct types exist in every office. While some of their cubicles should be padded, others should have doors that lock from the outside. But since that would damage the overhead budget, here's a heads up on some new and exciting personalities you will undoubtedly encounter. Sometimes your most important friend at the office could come in the least likely of places.

CHAPTER 10

THE OFFICIAL TITLES

The Mail Room Guys

THESE GUYS ARE YOUR ONLY HOPE FOR COOLNESS. They're the last line of Corporate. Like most offices, the guy who delivers the mail will be the most hip-hoppin' guy in the office, who smokes the most pot and sniffs the most white out. There should be a certain "whattup" between them and you that will result in your being able to send personal parcels across the country via overnight delivery at no charge. Mission accomplished.

You can always rest assured that the mail-room guys will be a bit thuggish, with hip-hop blasting on a bad stereo. You may even walk in on them rolling up a joint every now and then. Beware of any of these guys who promote their own nickname. T-Dog and Big Willie are going nowhere fast. The higher up the ladder you go, the fewer nicknames you'll hear. The mail room is full of T-Dogs. T-Dog will never make VP.

Befriend the guys in the mail room though; they're probably the best people in the office. But also remember that they are the mail-room guys, and associating with them while around the big-wigs will not be in your best interest. Be chummy with them—but only in the mail room—away from the bosses and gossipy cliques.

Office Managers

The office manager is a peculiar position. This is someone who does absolutely zero creative or thinking work. This job is in no way at all related to the actual trade of the company. His or her job is just to manage the problems and daily aspects of the office, yet the only reason the person got the job is because he or she couldn't hack it on your level.

Granted, the Office Manager may make more money than an assistant, but his or her Promotion Potential is very limited. So while the Office Manager may make $5,000 more per year than you, he or she usually has nowhere to go but nowhere. This person will usually do a really bad job of running the office. Wherever you go, remember this is someone who wasn't smart enough to do the regular jobs at the office. So it will be frustrating because the Office Manager has the ability to make your Corporate Life easier, but he or she won't. Because the Office Manager is incompetent.

The IT Guy

These guys are a different species. Sure they're human. Sure they work in your office, but they are sooooo different. They think they're smarter than everyone else in the company, but it's fine to let them think this. In fact it will actually work to your advantage.

Befriend them. They are like the corporate drug dealers, and the Head Boss is like the DEA. The Head Boss will do everything in his or her power to prevent you from having the good software you really want. Which means you may have a firewall at work that prevents your computer from having RealPlayer and Kazaa. You can't watch movies or download music?

How absurd! You may not even be able to download Flash or Acrobat Reader! If you don't have those things, your computer life will be a boring hell. Here's why you have to befriend the computer techie guys, the "drug" dealers. They've got what you want. First, call them up and do a little lying. "I need RealPlayer in order to watch presentations on CD-ROM." Try to speak in their lingo as much as possible. Let them know that you know what the programs are called and mention words like "server" and "java" when applicable.

Second, play to their egos. Say, "You probably don't have this, do you?" They'll say "Yes, I have everything," and then they'll start to toot their own horn. Once you've got them doing that, you're golden. When no one else is around, have them sit at your computer and ask for a software fix. They may say, "Can't. Firewall." So challenge them. Say something like, "Firewall, huh. Hmm, you can't beat it?" And then just to prove that they can, they will. If, however, the IT guys are obstinate and still won't budge, at the very least you've now had this little buddy-buddy heart-to-heart that will undoubtedly help you in the future.

Unlike everyone else in the office, the IT guys actually DO know something that you don't, and at some point, you will need them. They are the only ones in the office who will have a rotating hierarchy position. When everything is working fine with the computers, they are the lowest ones on the totem pole. But when the server goes down, all bets are off. When someone's virus-infected computer has more worms than a tackle shop, the IT guys become the Corporate Superheroes, lying low in their geek disguise until someone cries for help.

The Receptionist

Their main job is to greet people with a smile. For that reason they're often mistaken for nice people. Receptionists have it bad because people in your office mistake the forced smile for friendliness, so they will always dump personal information on the receptionist under the mistaken belief that they're the most trustworthy. This is never the case. Receptionists see more dirt than Mr. Clean. That's why they're always smiling.

The Assistant to the Boss

By far the biggest ego in the office, at times even bossier than the boss. Early on you'll make the mistake of calling him a secretary, and the Assistant will quickly inform you that he actually prefers the title of "Executive Assistant." Unless it's Administrative Professional's Day (yes, believe it or not, Secretary Appreciation Day was changed to Administrative Professional's Day), then you have to come correct with a gift.

All day long Executive Assistants answer the phone and screen calls. Their sense of self-importance would be ruined if someone told their boss that he or she could get Caller ID for seven bucks a month. It's an amazing deal. It never makes mistakes, files its nails, sticks its gum under the desk, or calls in sick when it's hungover. The only difference between an Executive Assistant and Caller ID is that sometimes Caller ID comes with a promotional offer.

There are two types of Executive Assistants, and they can both affect your Promotion Potential. The more common variety exudes pure evil. They're intelligent but overly competent, and they have no need for you or your petty request to get some face time with a Boss. The other less common type are those who've worked their way up to this position and are more humble toward coworkers.

They'll get you into a Boss's office. While these two personalities are different, Executive Assistants all have one thing in common: They know your salary. They know the salaries of the people above you and the people below you, and chances are they've told others. The salary breakdown is important information that will give you leverage when it's time to ask for a raise.

Befriend the Executive Assistants, regardless of how horrible or tragic they may be. Slowly the head honcho will see that you are the one who gets along best with the Executive Assistants. It's important to understand the relationship between the bosses and their Executive Assistants. It's the most intricate pairing in the office. Executive Assistants are relatively low on the totem pole, yet they are privy to more information than any of the VPs or anyone in the entire office for that matter. If you can tap into this constant stream of information, the things you hear can benefit you in ways you can't even imagine.

The Consultant

The Consultant is a funny character you will no doubt encounter during your tenure. There is really nothing written about this person ever because basically it is a new position. There were no such things as Consultants in the seventies and the eighties. And then all of a sudden, my friends were graduating college and becoming Consultants. I would ask them, "What exactly does a Consultant do?" And they would tell me things like they would go into a company and figure out how to make the marketing team better. And I'd think to myself, *Why don't they just fire the marketing team and hire the Consultants?*

And basically that's the gist of what's going on here. Consultants will work with you; but at the same time, they don't work with you. They sneak into your company to do the job that your present employees are supposed to do but can't. So you hire Consultants. We had a Consultant come into our office once under the title of "Efficiency Expert." She was trying to figure out just what everyone in the office did and how important they were to the "team." After three weeks there, the Efficiency Expert handed in her results as to who was expendable and who was not. In the end, only one person was fired the next day—the Efficiency Expert. I guess she found out that it wasn't very efficient having an Efficiency Expert watching over our backs every day.

The Controller

This is fancy Corporate lingo for the office accountant. How they scored such a cool-sounding title is beyond me, especially because they're pretty low on the totem pole in terms of actually "controlling" the decisions that really affect the company. No one else in the office has a job title that sounds like the next Vin Diesel movie, but somehow they pulled it off. You don't see the head of Sony Music walking around calling himself the Chief Groove Enhancer.

The Controller keeps the books. He or she records transactions and assets, prepares financial statements, and supervises the payroll. While they know all of the company's assets, what they DON'T know is just how valuable an asset they can be to a newbie. Don't ever piss one off. They're the ones who can delay your paycheck, withhold your expense reports, or not approve them.

If you get along really well with the Controller, he or she will see to it that your paperwork runs smoothly. Problem with your expenses? "No problem!" The Controller will walk you through the process so that it never happens again or so that it can be expedited as soon as possible. If you're on bad terms with one, however, you'll get an, "Oh, gee, I don't know what happened to your receipts. Can you send them again? Oh wait, I had the originals. Oh well!" Luckily, you made copies. You *did* make copies, didn't you?

Interns

Remember the first internship you had when you where so scared and terrified after one day of work that you never bothered showing up again? Well, guess what? The Ferris wheel just came full circle. Now you have some delicate young innocents looking for you to teach them the ropes about the business.

Interns are easily influenced. They form impressions quicker than plaster of paris. After their first day, they know who in the office they like and don't like. If they like you, they'll do things for you. You can then start giving them all the tasks you don't want to do. You'll never have to schedule a meeting or draw up an expense report again. That said, you should always treat Interns with respect and make them feel important whenever possible. In a few years this kid could be your boss.

If you are just starting out at your job, you're pretty much still an Intern yourself. You have to look up to the Office Manager for help in getting started and learning about the job. The only difference between you and the Intern is that you can't quit. You don't have a dorm room to crawl back to. Instead, you've got rent, bills, and a drinking habit that you picked up over the last four years.

CHAPTER 11

THE "UNOFFICIAL" TITLES

The Human Clock

EVERY OFFICE HAS ONE, THE PERSON IN THE office who knows EXACTLY how many minutes are left until it's time to go home. His watch is synchronized to the office clock. "Only six more hours till we're outta here!" Usually it's the guy who's more stressed than the fracture in Joe Theisman's leg. He hates his job, and he's dying to get out of the office.

The irony of the Human Clock is that this is probably the one person in your office with the least going on outside the office. What is this guy in a rush to go home and do? How sharp does his samurai sword collection really have to be? Someone should tell him his ant farm is self-sustaining. If you want to have some fun with the Human Clock, invite him to Happy Hour. Get a pitcher, get your drink on, then look at your watch and tell him "fifteen minutes till we're shitfaced!"

Don't confuse the Human Clock with his close relative, the "Calendar." Calendar types label the days for you. When it's Thursday, they'll say, "Only one more day." When it's Monday, they'll just shake their head and say, "Monday." When it's Wednesday, they'll want to go celebrate because it's, "Hump Day," halfway to Friday. And of course, on Fridays, they announce, "Thank God it's Friday!" As if you didn't know. They also keep track of the holidays, too. "Only nineteen more days until Thanksgiving holiday," they'll say.

The Sloth

If you are the Corporate version of a swan dive, the Sloth is a belly flop. This guy has no clue. He's not image conscious, and his Promotion Potential is so low you couldn't see it even if he got a raise. He gets by on personality alone, and chances are he's too big to even get on the ladder, much less climb it. Everyone likes him, but you never see him do any work.

While the Sloth may be a fun lunch break or drinking buddy, bad luck usually follows this guy around, so he'd best be avoided. This is the coworker who will get shit on by a bird during the company picnic. And chances are he won't even wipe if off, and someone will have to remind him that he's not a rhinoceros on the Discovery Channel.

Work Claimers

One day my boss asked me to type up some notes she had made in her notebook. I typed them up and put them on her desk in plain view for her to see. I didn't put a note on them or anything; she knew what they were.

But when I went back into her office a few minutes later, I saw the typed notes had been placed in an envelope and another young professional in my office had written, "Your notes," in her own handwriting. Even though I did the work, the fact that someone else put the notes in an envelope and wrote, "Your notes," on it would make it look like their work. Not unless I went in and took them out of the envelope (which you just can't do) or unless I told my boss I'd typed them up (to which she'd just say, "Yeah, I see them here. Point?") I wouldn't get credit.

The sad thing is that when a coworker claims your work, there's not much you can do to fight back. Tattling and silent treatment were fine in the fourth grade, but now these quality vices will damage both your Promotion Potential and your Corporate Identity. Instead, you just have to accept it and move on. It's going to happen, and when it does, it's best to not make a scene over it. Your star needs to always be on the rise, and you can't take the time to bring yourself down to this level.

The Pharmacist

During your first few days on the job, you'll have to fill out some serious paperwork. One of the forms you'll have to fill out will be for health benefits. You'll have to list your previous medical history to someone other than your doctor. You fill it out, turn it in, and off it goes to the insurance company. The process is so easy that you don't even realize that you've just turned in your form to the person who has the most interesting job in your office . . . the Pharmacist. Because before she seals up your form and sends it in to the insurance company, she gets to read it!

In large companies her job might be called Benefits Specialist. At a small company, she probably serves as the Office Manager. But in the end, she makes no more money than anyone else, and her confidentiality goes about as far as her telephone. The pharmacist knows your poison. She knows what ails you. She knows which newbies can't stay focused without first chowing on Ritalin; she knows who gets the Xanax; and she knows who can't crawl out of bed without their Prozac. She knows about your eczema and your chronic yeast infection. How? Because you indirectly told her by submitting your health care insurance forms to her.

Although it's definitely one of those best-kept Corporate secrets, let me be the first to let you in on some shocking news: pharmacists talk. They go to lunches, they go to drinks, they see people on their way to the vending machine. For reasons I can't explain, no one ever seems worried about this. No one ever talks about how much Pharmacists really know—except for the Pharmacists themselves of course.

I was pretty good friends with our office Pharmacist, and about a year ago I had a drink with her and one of her friends, another Pharmacist at a different company. Over dirty martinis, her friend started in about how much the new guy with the thyroid condition was costing their company in increased health expenditures. Then my Pharmacist friend told us about a woman at our company who was freaking out yesterday, most likely because her Zoloft had run out and she hadn't yet gotten a refill. She never referred to the woman by name, but I knew exactly who it was from her description. I couldn't believe how casually it came up in their conversation. Thank God she didn't talk about my crabs . . . I mean, uh . . .

The stress of the Corporate World is the reason many people need prescription medication. We don't have the luxury of running around the office like a bunch of A-list Hollywood celebrities, stringing ourselves out on little four-hour Vicodin vacations. In the real world, people have real problems. The Pharmacists are going to know these problems; and if you have personal issues, you should use discretion when dealing with them.

One-Uppers

A self-aware career assistant. All the rungs on the ladder have been snapped for these guys. They aren't going anywhere, and the worst part is that they know it. So they compensate, going the extra mile to make themselves look important. Anything to fluff their feathers, stick out their chest, and overall annoy you. Stay away from these people; they're bad news. I've seen Sears coupons with more redeeming value.

Luckily they're easy to spot, because the only way they can make themselves seem more important than you is by constantly one-upping everything you say. If you come in Monday Mourning talking about the Chili Peppers concert you saw over the weekend, they'll interrupt with a story about how they went backstage back in '94. If you talk about reading *CliffNotes* to *A Tale of Two Cities,* they've actually read the whole thing. Sometimes I can't wait to get promoted just so I can fire these guys.

ID Displayers

You know them, your coworkers who wear their badges around their necks on a chain or the ones who clip them to their belts or their pockets. They display their badge with a sense of pride, a sense of belonging. It's their medal of honor. Some even have a special leather case with a clear front that protects the ID and keeps it clean.

There was actually an Office Manager in my workplace who had a very innovative display for her ID. She kept her ID in the back pocket of her jeans. She's large and in charge, too; it's a big back pocket. Anyway, when she approached the ID swiping machine (it's touch sensitive, you just hold the ID up near it, and the security doors open) she just leaned her butt up against the wall and the doors opened. It was clearly the best move in the office.

Foreign Exchange

There will be someone in your office who is automatically assumed to be cool because they come from a distant land. Maybe it's a foreign country or maybe it's just a state where no one's ever been. Or a place no one's ever heard of. Whether it's Florence or Fayetteville, these workers will automatically be welcomed into any of the corporate cliques because they're a little different, and this makes that person seem "edgy."

I've seen a guy get promoted out of the mail room, and I swear it was because he was from Switzerland, talked with an accent, and wore tinted yellow sunglasses. He didn't have to be smart; but he stood out from the rest; and that got him noticed faster. So don't get upset when Devlin from Ireland makes VP before you; sometimes that's just the way it goes.

Late Bloomers

These are the people who weren't the least bit friendly to you when you first arrived on the scene. In fact they were probably worse than that; they might have been outright rude to you.

I remember when, my first day on the job, I walked up to a girl who was young and sitting in the Intern section, introduced myself, and asked her to make some copies for me—assuming she was an Intern of course. But she just looked at me with an, "Uhhh, get out of my face, newbie," look. Not an, "Oh, sorry, I'm not an intern. I'm Barbara, nice to meet you. Here, let me show you who the Interns are." It was my first day of work.

Then a few months into the job, once everyone else has accepted you and you may just be part of the "in-crowd," this same Late Bloomer who didn't take to you very well in the beginning now wants to be your "buddy" at work. You'll just be sitting in your cubicle, working, and she'll mosey on up with nothing better to do and set a magazine, a file, or a book down on your ledge and start flipping through the pages. Chances are it's not this book she's reading because then she'd know I'm holding an everlasting grudge because she made my first couple of weeks miserable.

Dieticians and Maternity Moms

You've seen 'em both. They're the ones who clog up the kitchen freezers with Lean Cuisines and Weight Watchers. They eat rice cakes at their desk. "Dieticians" are the people in the office who are constantly on a diet. Dieticians won't be the smartest people in the office because everybody knows frozen meals can't actually make you lose weight. Have you ever actually seen anyone "Lean" eating this cuisine? It's still a Salisbury steak smothered in buttery gravy; how is this going to make you lose weight! If Healthy Choice was actually healthy they'd be selling them in the produce section next to the fruits and vegetables. If Weight Watchers actually made you lose weight, they'd go out of business.

Maternity Moms are my favorite people in the office. They're laid back and easy to get along with because they know that in a couple of months, they'll get to take a long vacation. When coworkers get pregnant, it's like they have Diplomatic Immunity. They can now do the bare minimum to get by, and it doesn't matter if they screw up. They have nothing to lose. They know that no matter what happens, they get a paid vacation and an option to return to work after a few months of bringing up baby.

Kitchen Vultures

After a couple of weeks at your job, you'll notice that the same person is always in the kitchen whenever you go in. Whether it's a morning coffee run or a postlunch water cooler fill up, the same guy is in there, maximizing efficiency by eating as many snacks as possible in the shortest amount of time. Kitchen Vultures are the Corporate homeless: they work for food. From the chocolate chip bagels on the plate by the sink to the little bags of cheese nips stored next to the coffee filters, the Kitchen Vultures have a mental inventory of everything in the kitchen.

When you're in college, it's easy to spot who will grow up to become the Kitchen Vultures. At the end of every party, these were the esteemed group of individuals that no one really knew who would always roll in late at night and head straight for the kitchen, devouring everything in their sight. Half-empty beers and half-smoked cigarettes were their sustenance, and a bowl of Dorito crumbs could keep them busy for hours.

Kitchen Vultures are the ones who steal your food from the fridge. Even if your name is on something (though I highly suggest you not bring your own food to the office), they'll be sure to clear out the fridge at the end of every month. When you see Barbara in Human Resources scarfing down an egg salad sandwich with your name on it, you'll know you've been officially initiated into the Corporate World.

The Vultures are basically a harmless flock, but they're not the best ones to befriend. With all the implicit rules governing eating both in and out of the office, you can be sure that the bigwigs will eventually notice if someone spends all their time in the kitchen.

The Vultures aren't a particularly productive group, and you don't want your Corporate Identity to reflect this negative trait. Unless, of course, your company stocks the kitchen with Mrs. Fields Cookies and Swiss Cake Rolls. This advice cannot compete with that.

The Backup Disk

This is the most anal person in your office. These people are so organized that they don't have a single folder labeled "Miscellaneous."

Backup Disks are key allies; you need them on your side. If your computer crashes, if you lose a document or memo, you know they'll have it in their color-coded, meticulously organized filing system. When your desk is too messy and you can't find that one piece of paper you need right away, guess who will have a copy? You can have access to these files as long as you stay on their good side.

The Senator

The master of office politics, the Senator knows how to use every situation to his or her advantage. You can't trust the Senator with any gossip, trade secrets, or weekend antics. This person has his or her hand in everything around the office, whether it's a good in with the IT Guy or a few inside jokes with the Executive Assistant. These are slick cats; and even if you try your hardest, you'll never get any dirt on them.

Senators like to instigate. They will pretend to be friends with everyone in the office, but really they have only one true friend— themselves. They thrive on creating chaos by either generating false rumors or purposely leaking news to the office gossips. While they will be responsible for stirring things up, they will never be the ones to stand up for a wrong or speak out against management. They're the ones who will find something wrong with the system and will point out that extra money is unquestionably being deducted from your pay, but they won't be the ones to question management on this. No, sir. They set you up to become the "mouthpiece," while they sit back and watch you get reprimanded.

The Narc

This is the brown-nosing character who can't be trusted with any information. Narcs follow one step behind the Head Boss. They like to ask questions in meetings, and some of the more daring ones will even suggest that the meeting begin with a round of applause for the Head Boss's latest accomplishment. Kissing up to the Head Boss is their primary reason for being there.

Never, and I stress, NEVER, criticize higher authority when in the presence of a Narc. If you talk shit about one of your bosses and the Narc overhears, it's the first topic of conversation when he sees that boss in the vending area. Next thing you know you'll be getting a warning from Barbara in Human Resources.

Narcs come in all shapes and sizes. They can be anyone from an entry-level assistant all the way up to the second in command. And if they are second in command, guess how they got there? But also guess why they'll never be numero uno?

The Boss's Pet

Ever wonder what happened to that horrible teacher's pet you went to school with? Chances are they now they work in an office somewhere, sucking up to the Head Boss in all the wrong ways. In school the teacher's pet was never the student with the most intelligence, and in the Corporate World it is no different. These are the people who can't get the job done, yet they can do no wrong in the eyes of the Head Boss.

You're always covering up their mistakes so your entire department doesn't look bad. Who knows why this happens. Maybe they're holding a little bit of blackmail over the Head Boss; maybe they remind the Head Boss of an old friend, a new girlfriend, a daughter, a son he never had. Who knew he'd want a dumbass for a son? Regardless, get in good with the pets. Don't become friends with them—remember that they suck—just get in good with them.

The Drama Queen

They're easy to spot or, rather, hear. They are the ones you can always hear overdramatizing even the most mundane everyday tasks. And don't get me wrong, just because it's called "Drama Queen" doesn't mean it's reserved for females. There are tons of "Drama Kings" in the office. Nothing is ever uncomplicated to them because they put their spin on it.

Drama Queens crave attention. They are the coworkers who always have a small part (never a starring role) in the local theater group. Mind you, it's volunteer theater, and they're not actually getting paid to do this, yet it takes precedence above their real jobs, their paying jobs. These coworkers always announce to everyone that they have to leave early for "rehearsals" and constantly annoy you with invitations to come out and see their latest performance. Under no circumstances do you become chummy with these superstars, unless, of course, you enjoy spending your lunch going over lines for *Arsenic and Old Lace.*

Drama Queens weren't hired because of their superior intellect. Somewhere in their tenure at the company, they befriended the right person, and it is because of this friendship or connection that they are tolerated. While it's usually a distant relative of a boss or a boss's wife's best friend's daughter, they are protected from harm—and are usually harmless. This is the person who pretty much does whatever they want at the office—comes in late, takes two hours for lunch, leaves early—because they can. It's okay to be friendly with these people; just don't become their friend.

CHAPTER 12

YOUR "FRIENDS" AND "NEIGHBORS"

The People You *Say* "Hello" To

THE HELLO PEOPLE ARE PEOPLE YOU MAY HAVE met or worked with on something for a minute or two at one point a few weeks back, but since then you've never had anything to do with them again. So occasionally you'll pass them in the hall, and you'll say, "Hello," smiling at them. Then maybe later in the day the same thing will happen. This may go on for weeks, maybe even months. You may accrue a good five hundred "Hellos" with a person you NEVER talk to. Never.

The People You *Whisper* "Hello" To

Whisper People are those you see often in your building, but you never have had any real introduction to them nor have you ever worked with them. You may know who they are, but you can't assume they know who you are. Regardless, you don't technically know each other, but you pass each other in the hall or share an elevator and they seem nice so you whisper, "Hi." Again, you could accrue tons of these.

The People You Grin At

You're not even on a whisper, "Hi," status with the Grinners. They work in another company, but you ALWAYS seem to be going the same place they are. You arrive at the same time, you leave at the same time, you look up and see them sitting across from you when you sneak off to the Dim Sum Palace for lunch. You never deal with them, and you've never been introduced. So you just give them a little grin, sometimes a forehead raise, then you walk by them. And that's the extent of your relationship with the Grinners.

The Optimist vs. the Pessimist

Monday morning, it's pouring outside, and the Optimist employee is smiling anyway. Optimists are "people" people and "morning" people.

Pessimists are the bipolar opposites. They say things like, "I'm so tired," and, "Will this day ever end?" It's Friday afternoon, everyone just got a raise, and they don't crack a smile. You ask them how they're doing, and you get a story about their bad shoulder, their cat, and their migraine. A Pessimist typically has more negative energy than an electron generator. Break out the Kleenex every time this person starts talking.

Sometimes, when Optimists forget to take their medication, they temporarily switch over to the dark side. But don't worry, this sudden shift will be short lived. The pills will kick in soon enough, or else the shrink will simply up the medication. Regardless, order will soon be restored.

Office "Friends"

You're not going to get that promotion unless you are well liked around the office. You will have a certain hierarchy of the level of comfort you feel with people at work. Most of the people you'll get along with pretty well. These will be your "work" friends—not to be confused with your "friends." You don't call your real friends your "real friends." They are only your "real friends" because now you have "office friends."

Do you call your office friends over the weekend? No. Why? Because you don't like them. You pretend to. You laugh with them and talk with them about things. You feel concern for them. But you'd never phone them over the weekend. You don't even have their numbers at home. You don't call people you don't like. It's that simple. But these, unfortunately, are the people you hang out with and see a good forty times more than you do your friends or family.

Don't get me wrong. It's okay to have a friend or two at work. Just make sure it's only a friend or two. You'll need someone to complain to, someone to warn you of the calm before the storm, someone to have lunch with on slack Fridays. You will have all sorts of "friends" at work. The two most interesting kinds are your "temporary friends" and your "one-thing-in-common friends."

A "temporary friend" is someone who once a month you work with on a project, so for a few days out of each month you spend maybe thirty-five hours with them. But then for the rest of the month, you don't work with them. But you will see them around the office and remember that you worked together and really got to know one another, sort of; but now that you are on a break from each other, you really don't have anything to say except that your next project together won't start up for another three weeks. So you guys are on "temporary friend" status. The trick is to have a lot of temporary friends. Be on good terms with them, and they will like you. And you only have to spend a total of thirty-five hours a month with them. Let them spread the word that you're a good guy, and your Promotion Potential goes up.

The "one-thing-in-common friend" is someone with whom you discover you have something in common. Perhaps you were both somewhere at the same time (a concert, a movie, a restaurant) and it's your only topic of conversation. Maybe outside of work you have a friend in common, so they'll always say, "Talk to Scott lately?" And you'll probably say, "No, I haven't talked to him in forever. I gotta call him." You probably don't even like Scott that much. In fact you probably despise him, thereby pretty much despising the "one-thing-in-common friend." With friends like these, who needs friends?

PART SIX

---

*CONGRATULATIONS, YOU'VE
JUST BEEN PROMOTED*

In the working world, the people that you think are on your team are really the ones who are your competition. Workers at Microsoft, believe it or not, are NOT in competition with workers at Apple. On the contrary, workers at Microsoft are in competition with workers at Microsoft, and workers at Apple are in competition with workers at Apple. Jim in Marketing might be your pal, and you guys might have lunch together and grab a brew every once in a while; but if Jim does a better job than you, he's getting your promotion. Jim is therefore not your friend.

Not every job and office is like this. Some jobs and companies have a ceiling, a glass ceiling if you will. You can see the top, but you can't get there. If this is the case, there is no need for competition. If there is just one director of your department and everyone else is in middle management making $35,000—then you don't have to worry about competition. It's only in companies where someone who does the same job that you do might get paid $10,000 more per year for reasons that are way beyond your comprehension.

Ever seen a group of pigeons fighting over a single, small piece of bread? Promotions take a lot of hard work, ingenuity, time, suffering, and humility. While all of these may apply to your first day on the job, a promotion does not happen overnight. It often takes years before you're offered a chance to take it to the next level, so here're some hints that will help you rise to the top:

CHAPTER 13

INCREASING YOUR PROMOTION POTENTIAL

Congrats on a Job Well Done!

BELIEVE IT OR NOT, YOU WILL RARELY SEE OR HEAR that compliment. In fact if you do see it, you will get it via e-mail. Compliments are no longer verbally expressed, not when you can now get sued for giving someone a pat on the back. This isn't school anymore where you do your work and get a grade back immediately that says "A+! Great Job!" Now you do your job and it's expected; don't do your job and you get an e-mail equivalent to the teacher's, "Please see me," that reads, "Stop by my office when you have a chance." And what sucks is that the rest of the world isn't really like this.

Take for instance, the fast-food industry. How many times have you gone in and ordered a plain hamburger, and yet when you leave they've given you a burger with cheese, ketchup . . . or even worse, mustard? They got the one thing they were supposed to do wrong. Their sole job is to take your order properly, and they made a mistake. Now think about how many times that has happened on a similar level—maybe the cashier at the grocery store doesn't know the price of something, or someone somewhere charges you the wrong amount. Maybe the doctor's office messed up your appointment time.

Think about all of the times people have screwed up in dealing with you on their job. Now think about this: if you make a mistake, chances are you're fired. It's OK for the cashier at Wendy's to mess up twenty-five, maybe thirty times a day. These places serve thousands of people a day. If they screwed you over in one minute, think about how many times they erred over the course of an eight-hour day?

In the Corporate World, you're allowed to screw up once. But don't EVER let it happen again. If you mess up more than once a year that's not a good sign. You'll be labeled a fuckup. That's because there are different standards for all different workplaces. There are also different standards for people in your workplace. That's right—you can take sexism, racism, equal opportunity, age discrimination, affirmative action, and throw it all out the door in the Corporate World. Fact is—maybe you'll get hired for one of those reasons—but if you can't take the heat, like Coolio says, you'll have to get your ass out 'da kitchen.

Getting a Raise

If you've worked in the same place for longer than a year, you've done a reasonably good job, and your company has invested time and money to train you, it's time to ask for a raise. Asking for a raise is easy; getting the raise is the hard part. But there are a few ways to guarantee a salary increase. The job market is always competitive; and if you've already been trained in a certain skill, your superiors will be reluctant to see you go. Not because they like you, but because they've invested in you. Your stock is rising, you're a walking bull market, and they can't bear to let you go because you're probably making them an obscene amount of money. So chances are you'll be rewarded if they see you looking elsewhere.

There are two main ways to ask for a raise, both are effective and it really depends where you work and for whom. Consider them both and utilize the one that makes the most sense:

1. THE STRAIGHT AWAY

Schedule a time to meet with the Head Boss, wear the snazziest thing in your wardrobe, your best shoes, polish yourself head to toe, and get ready to do battle. Sit down with him or her, offer a firm handshake, and outline the many ways in which you contribute to the company. Set yourself apart from the rest; list your past accomplishments and future goals. Say you love the company and look forward to a long and rewarding relationship at this place of business. Be careful not to laugh when you say this.

Once you've laid the groundwork, explain to this boss that you're only grossing $500 after your rent, car payment, student loans, and other expenses. Let him or her know that an annual net profit of $500 isn't cutting it. You're not saving for the future, and you're not living the life you've envisioned. It may sound pathetic, but he or she will actually be impressed to see a youngster planning for the future and looking ahead. Regardless, you've laid out your argument as best you can, offer a concluding handshake, and then wait for the augmented salary to roll in.

2. THE PASSIVE AGGRESSIVE

Not all bosses will be as receptive as the imaginary one listed above. If the only face time you ever get with the Head Boss is the huge self-portrait in the lobby you have to walk past every day, you may have to take a more hard-lined approach to supplementing your income. To pull this off, you'll need a friend you can trust.

Have your friend put in a call to your supervisor, pretending to be a high-ranking boss at a rival company. If your friend wants to use a pseudonym, make sure he doesn't pick a joke name. Seymour Butz won't get his call answered, and chances are, your friend will also start laughing. Pick a literary reference like John Yossarian or Don DeLillo since it's a safe bet the Head Boss has probably never had the time to read a book (they watch movies though so don't use Gordon Gecko or Colonel Kurtz). Then instruct your friend to call this boss and say that he's just received your résumé and it looks fantastic. Your friend is therefore interested in hiring you to come work at his company, but he just wants to know a little more about you.

Upon hearing this, the Head Boss will immediately confront you, demanding to know why you're looking for another job. At this point, you're back to the $500 speech outlined above. Only this time, you're tone is more somber, to the point of embarrassment. You didn't know how to ask for a raise properly, you were too embarrassed, but you're simply not making ends meet. The more pathetic you sound, the more he will take pity on you and tell you to allow some time while something gets worked out. He should NEVER fire you over this, it's a guaranteed boost in income, and all you have to do is grovel for thirty seconds. Make sure you donate a portion of your raise to buy dinner for Yossarian.

An important thing to know about salaries and raises is the Scale. Every company has one—acknowledged or not. It's the amount of money by which the company is willing to increase your salary. Basically what you need to understand is the range in which everyone else around you gets paid. If you are starting off as an assistant in a big city you are probably making between $26–28k a year, unless you're working for a bigwig. Most likely your next raise will be in the $35k area. But if you ask for that you won't get it. You have to highball them. Ask for $10k more so that you can give them a chance to say no and then come back with $7k ($35k total) to which you can happily agree.

If you're already making $35k, the important thing to remember is you should be two raises away from $50k, meaning that your next raise should get you somewhere in the 40s so that the raise after that puts you over the $50k line. After that I have no experience and cannot tell you a thing about how negotiations will work to raise your salary from $50k to $75k. Fact is if you're already in that ballpark, you're probably not reading this book.

Be Perceptive

Doing a good job isn't always as simple as just doing a good job. You can be a whiz at what you do—a genius—but surviving among your peers is going to take more than just brains and talents. You've got to be able to look around and realize your environment. It's been said that in the armed forces you learn job skills and training. I always wondered to myself how the hell a guy who spent sixteen months in the jungles of Cambodia, hiding in swamps for six hours at a time, eating earthworms for protein, would excel in the Corporate World. After spending a few weeks in the Corporate trenches, however, I realized where the two meet. The Corporate World is all about assessment, plans, practicality, and understanding your environment. If the armed forces don't teach you that, then you're in the wrong army.

In the Corporate World, you have to look at your environment and figure out how you fit in. It doesn't matter if you're a numbers wunderkind working in an accounting firm if no one likes you and never wants to promote you. If you always need help with projects, if you can't do anything without direction, if you can't make up your own plans for doing something—you're just going to become a bottom feeder. Open your eyes to the office around you. Take off your blinders and examine EVERYTHING. Examine not only the physical attributes of the office—but examine the people and their moods. Look deep inside your coworkers and figure out what the hell is going on.

Remember that most of them are humans, too, and some things they say might be either a direct reflection on or projection of something that's happening outside the office. They might be constipated, their wife could have missed her period, their husband could have stumbled home drunk again—you have no idea. So take note. Don't ever approach anyone the second they walk in. Give them a minute to breathe, a minute to settle in, a minute to check their voice mail, and a minute to check their e-mail.

There was a lady in our office who had no perception. She was labeled "the Terrier." She got to work thirty minutes earlier than everyone else, and no matter the situation, she walked the halls harassing everyone as soon as they came in. It could be twenty-five degrees and snowing outside. Your car might have stalled, you might have stepped in dog shit, you forgot to eat breakfast and you're hungover—and this lady will be nipping at your heels, asking if you read the e-mail she sent you last night. God forbid she should give you a little space. If you have this lady in your office, don't let her make you feel like a slacker. You're not. She's just being annoying. In fact I guarantee everyone else in the office thinks it, too.

Take a deep breath and verbally pet your coworkers who lack perception. Tell them you'll get to it as soon as possible. They might want to keep talking and talking—and unfortunately you have to let them. Because that's what they do. But you can still keep walking to your desk and take off your jacket and turn your computer on and straighten up. You do what you have to do.

Don't Fall Asleep

No matter what it takes, you must stay awake and alert during the day. Or at least give the appearance that you are awake and alert. Whether you need a triple latte or a pack of Camels to get make it through, no boss wants to promote someone who doesn't seem focused and inspired by the job. Sure, it's hard—especially after last night's body shots at the Coyote Ugly—but it's just like driving while tired; close your eyes for just one second and its good-bye road, hello tree.

Keeping yourself happy at work is of the utmost importance. You have to realize that work is going to get you down. That's OK—if you expect it to happen, you'll be prepared for it. So you'll need to do things that can supplement your lack of enjoyment at work.

Stimulation is good at work. Your surroundings can become so mundane that even the slightest glimpse at a Christina Aguilera or Tom Cruise screen saver can send your endorphins flying through the roof. Let's say you sit at your cubicle all day and stare at your computer. Likelihood that you'll see anything other than your corporate surroundings for nine straight hours is pretty bad.

So take breaks and go into different worlds. Go to another floor in the building and walk around their floor. Sure you'll get blank, curious stares from most of the people there, but who cares! The fact is you're dressed like them, you look like them, and chances are, there probably is a "you" somewhere on this floor. Take a quick lap and then head back up to your floor. You were only away from your desk for three minutes, but in that time period you forgot all about how miserable your coworkers, your working conditions, and your job are—you got to see someone else's.

If you're not up for that type of exposure, just go to the vending area downstairs and stare at the Cokes, Sprites, root beer, and snacks. They're creative and colorful and fun to look at. They're light, dark, hot, cold, taste, caffeine, spice, flavor—they have meaning.

Staying awake would seem like common sense, but surprisingly that's not always the case. I had a friend in high school who took a summer internship in the office of an unnamed Republican senator from Virginia. Although my friend was a Democrat, he knew it would help his high school transcript, and college was the only party he really swore allegiance to anyway. So he took a job pushing paper and filing memos in hopes that the esteemed senator would sign a fluff letter of recommendation at the end of the summer.

It turned out to be different from what he expected. The job called for long hours, and the senator was never actually in the office. One day, after a long night out in Adams Morgan (a D.C. hotspot), my friend headed back to the office and crashed on the senator's leather couch. Of course the next morning was the one day that the senator decided to show up. Imagine his surprise to find my buddy passed out on his couch. That's nothing compared to my buddy's surprise when he opened his eyes to find a pissed-off U.S. senator towering over him. Needless to say, at the end of the summer the senator refused to write him a letter of recommendation.

Tips for Surviving the Hangover

I don't work for the health insurance company, so I know you consume more than one beer or glass of wine per month. And on occasion, one will lead to many more, and next thing you know that great buzz from the night before is suddenly the annoying buzz of your alarm clock. In college you could sleep off a nasty hangover, but times have changed now that you have a job. You work now, and you HAVE TO GO.

So you have to learn how to cope with the hangover. And you have to know which hangover calls for which remedy. There are basically three kinds of hangovers when at work:

1. THE PLAIN OLD-FASHIONED HANGOVER

This is the kind you get when you go out with your coworkers. Your head is pounding, your stomach is churning, you're nauseated, you can't eat, you can't work, you can't drink anything . . . you just stare at your computer. Don't waste a good sick day on this type of hangover. Take an Aleve; you'll feel better after lunch.

2. THE "STILL DRUNK AT WORK" HANGOVER

This is the kind you experience when you go out with your "real friends." This is when you were so drunk the night before, and you stayed out so late, that when you woke up in the morning, you were still drunk. Even while you showered, got dressed, and drove to work. If you're a woman, putting on makeup turns into a dangerous afterthought that combines sharp eyeliner and 65 mph traffic. If you're fortunate enough to arrive at the office in one piece, you'll soon realize it's not the best place to be when you're still drunk. You reek of alcohol, you have a short attention span, you're talking about random things, and you look like a mess. To offset this predicament, spray on plenty of cologne or perfume before you leave your house. Brush your teeth twice, gargle with mouthwash, and soap and shampoo yourself well. Your body is going to be giving off a strong stench of alcohol, so you need to do the best you can to limit it. Chew gum and eat mints during the day, too. The last thing you need is someone smelling the booze on you.

3. THE "STAY AT HOME" HANGOVER

This will happen two to three times a year. The problem is diagnosing it. Of those two to three times, you're going to try and go to work the first time. Bad move. You spend more time in the restroom than at your desk. You won't be productive—and you could cause problems for the future. You might do or say things that a normal, healthy You wouldn't. So just stay at home and suck it up. Look, the joy of the Corporate World is that they give you two weeks a year sick leave. Since you're not a kid anymore, chances are good that you're not going to be stricken with chicken pox or mono. You may get a strep throat or a cold—but you'll probably only use four or five sick days per year on actually being sick. Take into account the one or two you'll now use for your Stay at Home Hangover and you've still got five days left. Save those days to tack onto your one-week romp in Amsterdam, and all of a sudden you've got a twelve-day Eurorail pass.

Be careful *not* to leave trace evidence of your wild night out. Case in point, the hand stamp. Sure, when you were eighteen years old and using your fake ID to get into a bar, it was cool to show up at class the next day with a big black "Club Spank" stamp marked on your hand. But now you're Corporate. You don't want that on your hand. Sure it may be hard to scrub off, and sometimes it seems like they use Sharpie ink for the stamp, but find some Lava soap, alcohol, or nail polish remover. Use anything as long as you erase that puppy.

Occasionally you'll go out with your friends on a random Tuesday night and get totally obliterated. Come 3 a.m. you're still out getting trashed. The next day at work will be horrible, and you'll spend the day e-mailing back and forth with your friends. It'll be something like, "Damn, dude, no way am I ever gonna drink again on a Tuesday." "I know, no more of that." "Never again." "We're adults now." Those e-mail exchanges are a distant memory when the next Tuesday rolls around and you're looking for something to do.

Young and Spontaneous

What matters most at your company is your production. That's why age discrimination is prevalent in most offices. But guess what? It's not discrimination! The entire workplace has morphed dramatically over the years. Everything is now done on the Internet, via the computer, e-mail, fax, etc. Phone calls happen at lightning speed—the hard drive is the new file cabinet. And if you're over the age of forty-five, you're finding yourself increasingly at a loss. Watch the young kids these days fly through memos and files on the computer. Then watch the fifty year old. Sad but true. Sure, every company needs "white hairs" at the top, but middle management and executives are getting increasingly younger and younger. You couldn't have been born at a better time!

The most annoying person I've ever worked with was also one of the oldest. Although he was a partner in a large company with offices around the world, I have no idea how this guy got any work done. He didn't have a cell phone or a fax machine, and he didn't ever check his e-mail. He was fondly labeled "Fred Flintstone," and since he never came into the office, getting in touch with him was next to impossible. Whenever he was the last to hear about something, he always blamed someone else. If only he had taken the time to learn the newer technology, he could have been even more successful. And less annoying.

I love my parents, but I wouldn't hire them to work for me. I'd hire the young gun out of Georgetown, experienced or not. And I could pay him less! Plus, young people don't have kids, wives, families, cancer, surgery, carpal tunnel; they don't have to leave early; they don't have financial problems, new car payments, mortgages, or other issues. I know, I'm disgusting. But at the two biggest corporations I have worked at, the average age was probably around thirty to thirty-five; and EVERYONE, I mean everyone knew that, aside from the bosses, the worst two or three workers we had were the ones older than fifty. They just had problems, plain and simple. The best workers? The young guns. They'll say, "Wow, that kid is sharp! Who found him?" I guarantee this is a phrase you will hear on several occasions. Congratulations if you are that kid.

You're young. You should have no ball and chain. No lead weights dragging you down. You should be free of any sort of constrictions that might hold you back. Simply put, you are available to work 24-7 if needed. If the company needs someone to fly to the Galápagos Islands to work a deal, you're available. It could be Friday at 6 p.m., and if they need someone there by 8 a.m.—you go. All you really have to go to that night is Steve's twenty-third birthday party.

If you were a thirty-eight-year-old VP, you'd have a wife, kid, and sick grandmother to go home to, and there would be no way in hell you could leave on short notice. But you're not! You're you! And you're twenty-two! Or twenty-three! Or twenty-four! Whatever, you're going to the Galápagos Islands, baby!

It doesn't matter that the only reason they sent you is because you were their last resort. They still sent you. And they'll send you again and again, until you finally become "the person they send." Granted, it may never be the Galápagos Islands. It may be Newark. Or Omaha. Or it could just be downtown. Regardless, be ready— be available.

I worked at a job where travel was such an integral part of the job I actually kept a packed tote bag under my desk with a ready-to-go toiletries bag, change of skivvies, socks, and a nice shirt—just in case I got that last-minute call. Plus, who the hell would want to give up the opportunity to travel on someone else's dime? Not me.

Choosing What's Important

When you're young, you want a lot of things. You want money, you want success, you want opportunity, you want fun, you want everything. Well, it's no different when you get older either. You still want money (the only difference is now you NEED money), you still want success (only now that it's possible, you are slowly seeing it slip out of your grasp), you still want opportunity (only now they are probably giving it to the person below you . . . or worse—the new guy), you still want fun (only now you're old so you can't have fun), and you still want everything (only all you might have is NOTHING).

As you get older you begin to realize these all go hand in hand with each other. You realize that if you've got money, you've probably got success; and if you've got success, you've probably got money. If you've got both of those things, then you probably had opportunity and may still have it. And with all of those things comes fun. And once you complete the equation with fun—well, you probably have everything.

Work at one part of the equation at a time. I know when I first was starting out in the workplace, I was so set on trying to make money and succeed that when I went on vacation I couldn't really enjoy myself. I would sit on a lounge chair and start writing, or I would try and brainstorm, or look for jobs or figure out ways to better myself. Once I became comfortable where I was in the working world, I was able to enjoy my "fun" a little bit more. Vacations truly became vacations, not a time for me to work on extra curricular projects. And once I had fun I became more motivated and things got better at work.

I had a friend who used ALL fourteen of his vacation days and all ten of his sick days every year. Tack that on to the five corporate/national holidays he got during the year and this guy was taking a full month off each year. He would take off random Mondays and Tuesdays without a worry. But believe me, he'll be worried when he's twenty-nine, and he's still not where he wants to be.

Although you are absolutely entitled to these days off, and you should take some time off if necessary, don't use ALL of your sick time. Even more important, DON'T USE ALL OF YOUR VACATION TIME. You may think I'm crazy for saying this, but when you're thirty-five you'll thank me. You don't need all of that time when you are young. First of all, you shouldn't need ten sick days. You should need at most five, including time off for the Stay at Home Hangover. Never take more than two days off in a row. If you get sick more than two days in a row—you need to quit smoking (you will notice in the Corporate World that only smokers get sick chronically).

Taking a vacation can work against you because your coworkers will be working for you. When you're gone, someone else is going to have to do your work. They might do it better. Or your boss might realize that they don't need you that much. Or the project you REALLY wanted comes up right in the middle of your five-day bender in Costa Rica. You have to decide very early on who you are. Are you a worker? Or are you a partier? I say be a worker—because at some point it will allow you to be a partier. Being a partier never allows you to be a worker.

Corporate Evaluations

It's possible that once a year you're going to have to evaluate yourself. Your superiors will ask you to list everything you do on both a daily and weekly basis. They'll want to know what you do, how you go about doing it, and how long it takes you. They cover everything, right down to the last specific detail. Unfortunately, it's not so simple as giving yourself an A. If it were—you'd be giving yourself your own raise and promotion.

I remember in high school my teacher gave us all a paper to write, and then told us to evaluate and grade the paper on our own. I question myself now as to why I only gave myself a B+ back then. I was a C student in that class, giving myself an A+ should have been a no-brainer. If I don't give myself an A, why should anyone else? In the end it's the grades that matter, not how you got them (unless you got caught cheating). In the Corporate World, where the stakes are higher, you've got to symbolically give yourself that A+.

When they ask you about your job, tell them EVERYTHING that you do. Mention everyone you talk to and how long you work on certain projects. Similar to writing a good résumé, you should add color when appropriate. Don't say you just "made copies" when you could say that you "collated and organized the data." It sounds much better that way.

While these evaluations may seem like an exercise in futility, the bigwigs take them very seriously. In fact they look at these forms as a direct reflection of your work, so it's best to put in some effort. This is the one time when you're given extra work that you can use to your advantage. When I last had to evaluate myself I turned in a beautiful two-page report, properly spell checked, and neatly aligned. Some of my items were in list format, others were in paragraph form.

I spent a lot of time on it and not only made it look good but made it sound good. One of my coworkers waited till the last minute to do his—literally. On his way out the door on the day it was due, he quickly wrote a few things down, complained about one or two things, and submitted it. He didn't even spell check, which made it obvious that he put no time into it. In just two minutes he managed to lower his Promotion Potential. Meanwhile, I got an e-mail receipt back from the boss who was coordinating the evaluations in which she thanked me for doing such a great job on mine, getting it in early, and making it easier for her to read.

Granted, there are a few traps you should avoid when filling out your Corporate Evaluation. If they ask you to say where you need improvement—DON'T SAY A WORD! You don't need improvement on anything as far as they are concerned. You are a superior modern-day worker. In fact say that you've got a really good grasp on things and you don't NEED improvement in any facets of your job, only that you look forward to improving your skills and abilities as you challenge yourself with higher goals and learn how to do other jobs within the company.

They also might ask you to evaluate other people or the company as whole. Be VERY careful with this section. This is something they will file forever on you, so watch what you write. Be very general and positive. This isn't the time to play Mr. Fixit with all of the company's problems. You should never express negativity with regard to your coworkers or job, but if you are going to do it, do NOT put it in writing. Simply express it verbally after seriously calculating what you will say, or else you will find yourself explaining to Jim in Marketing why you wrote that he should be fired.

Recommending Somebody

Be careful if and when you recommend somebody for a job. Remember how hard it was for you to get a recommendation? Let alone three? Well, don't make it that easy on someone if he needs you to help him get a job. Obviously, if you know him very well and know he is competent, it's Ok to hook him up. But that's not always the case, especially with your friends.

I had a friend who asked me to get her a job at my company. She had just been fired from her job (red flag!) and was desperate. I placed a few calls and submitted her résumé to the proper people. I made a couple of follow-up calls on her behalf, put in a good word, and got her a job interview. Then she forgot to show up. It made her look bad, but more importantly, she left me out to dry and damaged the Promotion Potential I'd spent years suffering to attain.

I also once recommended a friend of mine to a graduate school program where I had a connection. I got him into the program, and then he flunked out. It's not always going to happen that people will perform poorly when you recommend them, but it's certainly something to keep in mind. Nowadays, unless I am 100 percent positive that this person will excel at whatever I say they will, I usually give very generic recommendations via phone like, "I can't vouch for this person's academic ability, but I can say he or she is a dear friend, a good person, and I think if hired would make a great addition to your team." That way I say "if hired" rather than "please hire" this person. Then it's not on me when they show up for their First Day wearing ripped jeans and a college sweatshirt.

CHAPTER 14

RISE OF THE MACHINES

Corporate Darwinism

REMEMBER ALL YOU LEARNED ABOUT SURVIVAL OF the fittest? Sure, Darwin was talking about animal vs. nature or animal vs. animal. I'm sure he never imagined the comparison of human vs. modern work surroundings. But it still applies. Only now, it's you against the Xerox machine. It's ironic that everyone in the Corporate World calls it a "Xerox" machine when Xerox is only one of many companies that do document processing. And since their copiers are so fucking expensive, most places will never actually have a Xerox machine. They'll have the cheaper versions. Don't believe me? What copier advertises the most and is the most embedded copier image in your brain? Xerox. Now go look and see what kind of copier your office uses. I'll bet you a box of Kleenex® or Q-tips® that it's not Xerox®.

I used to work for a boss who never used a computer. I thought I could use this to my advantage because surely someone who is intimidated and scared of computers will probably think that they are very hard to operate. It turned out, however, that he was a technophobe deviant. Rather than being scared of computers, he thought they were easy to operate and he therefore expected instantaneous results from all my coworkers. He would tower over me, demanding the investor "alpha list" (Corporate speak for "the list that is alphabetized"), and I had to show him how I had to cut and paste each one individually. It takes time. I couldn't just do it with a couple of mouse clicks. He would ask for impractical things. Everything he wanted took forever, and his directions were always unclear. You could be a mind reader and you still wouldn't be able to get a straight answer from this guy. We called him "Boardwalk" because of the way he monopolized our time.

Master the machines. We can put a man on the moon, but we can't invent a copy machine that won't jam. Learn the machines inside and out because as Murphy's Law would have it, the day you have a proposal due is the day the machine will break. You want to be able to fix it on the fly, but by all means you don't want everyone in the office to know that you know how to fix it. Then every time it breaks down everyone will be looking at you to fix it.

Mastering the machines gives you an edge and puts you ahead of the pack, and this skill alone will set you apart from the lesser coworkers who won't make the cut. There was a guy down the hall from me who tried to impress everyone with his new all-in-one fax machine/paper shredder combo. Sure it looked cool, but he never took the time to figure out how it worked. For the first week he thought someone was trying to send him confetti.

Signs You Are a Machine

I called my friend at work on a Saturday. He told me he was going into the office to work on some personal things, so I knew he wouldn't be answering his office phone. He told me to call at precisely 4:20 p.m. so that he would know it was me calling and would therefore pick up the phone. At 4:20 p.m. I called him; and even though we had already discussed that it was going to be me that was calling him, he subconsciously answered the phone by saying, "Marketing, this is Jim." He was a machine. Before I could even say anything to make him aware of what he had just done, I could hear him shaking his head. He knew what he had done. And as a veteran of the Corporate World, he wasn't happy.

The same thing happens to me. On many occasions I come home from work and plop down on the couch. Sometimes, before I call one of my friends, I dial "9" first to get an outside line. Other times, while I'm zoning out watching TV, the phone will ring. And even though I'm at home, I'll pick up the phone and say, "Sony Marketing," in my nasally business voice. Or better yet, sometimes I'll be so busy at work that when I call people and I let it ring, when they pick up I automatically say, "Sony Marketing," as if they called me. I'm a machine. I'm trained to answer the phone a certain way 95 percent of the time I'm on the phone, so that's how I answer it, no matter what.

Casualties of War

In your journey to the top, there will be those who don't make it. Poor performance, company cutbacks, and the occasional shooting spree are all factors that could lead to the dismissal of one of your fellow coworkers. And it's become common courtesy for those dismissed to use their e-mail Rolodex to send out the final, good-bye e-mail.

"It's been a pleasure working with all of you over the last two years. If you're ever in Nevada, look me up!" And then they give their "personal" e-mail and their phone number.

The fact is that no one will ever call this person, ever. Before you even have time to be sad (or happy) that you'll never see this person again, they'll bring in someone new. The wheel keeps on turning, and suddenly you're watching another deer in the headlights caught without keys, an ID badge, and a nice back-crack chair.

People will get fired for a myriad of reasons, and you have to be careful at all times. Walk on eggshells at the office. Everything you do, everything you say, everything you wear, be very careful. I worked with a girl who once got fired for inadvertently offending a minority group. She wasn't the best worker as it was, in fact, it was her lack of attention to detail that indirectly landed her a pink slip. She was an Office Manager in charge of ordering dinner on nights when the entire office was working late. Her method of letting everyone know that the food was there was to e-mail the staff. So one time she e-mailed the entire staff and accidentally left out one letter from a word. She left out the letter "D" from the word "Food." What she wrote was:

Dinner is here. Chinese foo in the kitchen.

A few people in our office had a problem with what they claimed was not an accidental slip of the finger on the keyboard but rather an ethnic slur. Needless to say, she was out of there before I had even finished my orange chicken.

Corporate rules are no different from the stupid high school rules prohibiting you from wearing a Marilyn Manson T-shirt or laws preventing you from saying things like, "I wish the president was dead." Every institution has its rules, and while you may be used to following the minimal rules at George Washington Carver High or Iowa State College, now you're at Corporate U. There's no cheerleading squad, and the basketball team consists of you and your cubicle mate shooting paper baskets into your trash can. Step back by the copier and it's worth three points.

When my company closed down, it was like the battlefield after Gettysburg. I was literally the last person to leave the office on the final day, and it was a horrible couple of months because every Friday would be the official last day for a bunch of employees. This meant that at the end of every week, I'd get at least ten "good-bye" e-mails from a fresh batch of Casualties of War. Two months of this, and I finally ran out of Corporate colloquialisms. The, "Nice working with you," and the, "It's been a pleasure," wore thin, and I felt bad because constantly saying good-bye to people actually wears on you after a while.

The exodus was really sad, and I took a moment to reflect on each one of my former employees when it was my turn to shut off the lights and lock the door behind me that final time. Of course, as a child who grew up watching lame sitcoms, I turned around one last time and sighed before closing the door for good. Roll credits.

You Are What You Work

At the end of the day, remember who you really are, not where you work. All too often we forget about that. If you work in computers— it's what you talk about. If you work in finance, you talk numbers. If it's fashion, you're talking about the latest styles and trends.

I lived in D.C. for four years, and everyone works and talks politics. You're hanging out at a bar and someone will hear you say something they agree with and they'll shout, "Hey, buy that man a beer! He's a Democrat!" And the whole bar will erupt. I lived in L.A. for three years and all anyone does is talk about the movies.

You'll find yourself immersed in a conversation about which "is your favorite AIDS movie, *Philadelphia* or *And the Band Played On?*" Someone will shout across the bar, "*And the Band Played On* was a miniseries!" and then everyone will erupt in a harmonious, "Hey!!!!" Followed by, "Buy that man a beer!"

It's inevitable to some degree, but try not to let work vocabulary creep into your otherwise normal speech patterns. The only thing mechanical about you should be your pencil. Sometimes you become such a machine that you start to use work metaphors. I knew a case manager whose entire way of speaking changed after a routine visit from the IT guy. All of a sudden he was stalking around the vending area, complaining that his underlings didn't have the "bandwidth" to meet an upcoming deadline. Who talks like this? Hopefully not you.

Corporate Myths

You've heard the stories about the young student from Harvard who took any job he or she could get in order to break into the biz. She'd start as a receptionist and work her way up to CEO. She was the operator, the desk clerk, or the maintenance worker who stayed around after hours and learned the tricks of the trade that made her the success story that she is now. This is all bullshit.

The Secret of My Success was a MOVIE. You can't be a mail guy one minute, then throw on a suit and make big-business decisions the next, only to get back on the elevator and change back into your mailroom clothes. It doesn't work like that. Especially today. Granted, you should take a job at the bottom if it's all you can get. Even if you start off in Marketing or Business Affairs for the company you want to be in, you can still slowly meet the people in the department you want to be in so that after a year you can transfer over there.

Right after college I wanted to work a development gig in the film industry, but the only things being offered to me were business affairs jobs for production companies that happened to have development departments. I was broke so I took a job anyway, but I let it be known that I wanted to switch departments as soon as possible. Every weekend I took home screenplays for one of the development VPs and wrote up reports so that he wouldn't have to read them. He loved this. Not only did he not have to do his work, but now he had more time to go out and get laid and do blow with his Hollywood friends. I made myself a valuable asset, and within three months he had me transferred into the department I wanted. Three months after that, he transferred into Rehab.

You have to make things happen for you. No one else will. Recently I read an article about an assistant at the magazine, *GQ*. He spent some time working there, only to realize he was miserable working in a cubicle, staring at a computer all day long, making $30k a year. So he began writing, a screenplay no less. The title? "Screw You *GQ*, I'm Going to Hollywood." And do you know what the end result was? He sold it, screwed *GQ*, and went on to Hollywood. I'm jealous. You should be, too. Because he didn't change from mailroom clothes into a suit and try and trick everyone. He simply did his job, then went home at night and put his dormant creative juices to work. Hopefully though, he was smart enough to figure out how to write some of it while he was at work!

PART SEVEN

CLOSING TIME

CHAPTER 15

WHERE DO WE GO FROM HERE?

The Layoff

WHY DO BAD THINGS HAPPEN TO GOOD PEOPLE? A philosopher once said you have to deal with the bad to appreciate the good. You don't want to brush your teeth in the morning, but you also don't want cavities. You don't want to eat breakfast when you feel nauseous, but its better than being hungry at your desk at 11:00 a.m. You don't want to graduate college in four years, but at some point you have to grow up. Some things in life are inevitable; and when economic times are tough, not every company will make it.

I've been in the Corporate World long enough to have completed the Corporate Trifecta: I've changed jobs, been promoted, and gotten laid off. I have friends who actually want to get laid off. When they hear their company is about to make another round of cutbacks, they ask their supervisors to put in a BAD word for them. They've heard all about the lavish severance packages, and for some reason, the government will actually pay you a $300-weekly Unemployment Stipend if you lose your job. They pay you to not work, as if that's some kind of incentive to find a job as soon as possible. I worked for a company that went bankrupt during a recession, and I was on the first plane to New Orleans. I went to Jazz Fest on a government subsidy. For four days Uncle Sam spoiled me on crawfish and jambalaya. Four days turned into two weeks, and when I got back there was a check in excess of $600 waiting in my mailbox. That's not a lot of money, but it was the first time in my life I'd ever been paid for doing absolutely nothing.

Don't get me wrong, getting laid off has a horrible stigma attached to it. It screams "failure" and "unlucky," and it's the kind of party-stopping word that will have minglers looking at their shoes faster than an untied shoelace. Layoffs are the corporate version of a divorce. You're the kid, and you have to sit around and listen to your boss tell you how it's not your fault. Not that you'd ever actually blame yourself anyway. If any of the higher-ups had actually paid attention to the cost report you'd circulated three months ago, your company might have been able to stay in the game.

These days, the word "Layoff" has replaced the word "Fired!" More often than not, if you do your job well enough, you will never be fired. You'll just be laid off. But it happens. Of course, you'll probably quit more times in your lifetime than get fired or laid off. When you quit, get fired, or get laid off, you need to be professional about it, even if it's a weird situation. Be an adult. Don't do the Jerry Maguire, "Who's coming with me?!" performance. In fact, one up them. Be cool. Let your employers make all the actions and decisions, you just follow their lead as appropriately as possible. Remember, at one point they actually hired you. Chances are you had them at hello.

On that same note, make sure you are always prepared to leave on a minute's notice, especially if you "need" to quit. Make sure the personal stuff on your computer is backed up on a disk of some sort at least every couple of weeks and keep the disk at home. As you can imagine, when I told my employers I was quitting to go work for my boss who had left for a new job and that I wasn't giving two weeks' notice, rather, I was quitting that day—they told me there was no need to stick around. Being that they had confiscated my computer already, I luckily had my digital life on disk. I wasn't getting anything back. I was as good as done.

The Restarting

Getting laid off is like getting a death row pardon from the governor. It's a temporary relief, but it only delays the inevitable. Soon enough you'll have to face the music and get another job. After a layoff during a bad economy, it once took me seven months to find a new gig, and the disorientation I experienced upon my return was a devastating shock to my system. Like a Union soldier trying to fight in World War II, I had stepped onto a completely different battlefield. Going back into the Corporate World was like nothing I'd ever seen before. The nation's economy had been in a freefall, and nothing could have prepared me for what I was about to see.

On my First Day I walked in for what I thought would be one hour and ended up staying for eight hours. They told me to come in just to look over my new contract; but as soon as I walked in, I was ushered to my new work station. I hadn't even seen a contract yet so I asked my new Human Resources Department. After some deliberation, the new HR lady produced a dirty, two-page letter that looked like it had been delivered by Pony Express. It seemed like a flimsy Employment Agreement and they didn't even give me a chance to read it.

"So are you ready now?" she asked.

"At my last job I had to sign a bunch of stuff and fill out a stack of forms. Do I even get benefits?" I begged.

"Sure. Ready now?"

"Does it matter that I'm about to go on vacation for two weeks?"

"We'll get someone to fill in. Ready?"

After reading the initial job description, I assumed this would be a cake job, but never in my life had I seen such a high-pressure environment. For lack of a better Corporate cliché, it was like everyone was doing the work of ten people. No one had the time to train me. When someone finally took the time to actually notice me standing there, it was brutal. It made Ethan Hawke's experience in *Training Day* look like a driver's ed class.

For my first task they had me write down all the logins and passwords for all the databases throughout the office. A couple of secretaries were showing me how to access the "Executive Calendar," but all I kept thinking about was my own calendar, and just how much my first week back on the job ruined all the events I had planned. I had to flake on my weekly Monday Happy Hour for the first time in half a year. Beer, wings, and football were no longer the focus of my life. Tuesday I had to cancel plans for a movie matinee, Wednesday I had to sell my tickets to a concert, and Thursday I had to push back my birthday.

In addition to forgetting what it felt like to get a paper cut, I had also forgotten how much my wardrobe would have to change to conform to the office dress code. For seven months I'd gotten by with the same two outfits; a black shirt with khaki pants and a khaki shirt with black pants. I never saw the same person for three straight days, so no one ever really caught on. But now it was different . . . I needed at least three new shirts—for next week.

As soon as I started training, it finally dawned on me that I was no longer a free man, and for the first time in seven months, Monday Mourning came around, my alarm clock went off, my stomach tightened, and nausea crept in. It was time to go to work.

Changing Jobs—The Final Clichés

The biggest difference between our working environment in the twenty-first century and that of our parents' is job loyalty. It no longer makes sense to be a company man. Sweeping advances in technology, improved retirement packages, and various incentive plans make it impractical to rise up in the ranks at a single company. New companies are rising like weeds in the concrete jungle. You no longer need to stay at the same firm for the next forty years until you reach retirement. It doesn't make sense to be complacent when a more interesting opportunity could be right around the corner.

When you leave a company under your own volition, it's always good to write a quick letter making your intentions known and giving official notice of your imminent departure. Corporate Etiquette dictates that this is done two weeks before your last day in order to give your company ample time to hire a replacement. Always give your company notice before you leave; it shows the bigwigs that you are a class act with an admirable Corporate Identity. While it may have worked for General Sherman, burning bridges may end up costing you in the long run.

Your letter doesn't have to be an amazing piece of literature. Just a couple of sentences about how much you've appreciated your experience working at the company, but you feel it is time to pursue a new challenge and opportunity. Never complain, whine, or apologize; just let them know you're leaving and you wish them the best.

A couple of years ago I got an interesting piece of mail. The Assistant to the Boss at the first company I had ever worked at had been cleaning out her files, and she found two letters I had written to her boss. One was a letter I had written during college asking for an internship. The second was dated almost five years to the day of the first one, and it was my "two weeks notice" letter. These letters served as a two-page microcosm of my Corporate Life thus far.

The first letter was very formal. I referred to the Boss as "Mr." and listed all the qualities I thought I could bring to the company, were he kind enough to grant me an internship. In the second letter, I called the boss by his first name, I told him it had been a pleasure working for him and learning from him, and I was confident our paths would cross again.

And sure enough, they did. On the second letter, my old boss had taken the time to write me a nice note, wanting to know what I'd been up to in the past year, and offering to help if there was anything I needed. Had I not written a "two weeks notice" letter, this contact would most likely have been lost forever.

It's tough figuring out when it's time to move on. Sometimes you'll just get the feeling that it's time for a new challenge. Other times you'll notice that no one at the company ever gets promoted. Whether it's because you've relocated to do the same job or you just don't feel satisfied by the same job, several times during your Corporate Tenure you will have to clear out your desk and say goodbye to your coworkers. While the circumstances that lead to this situation will always be different, it's amazing how the actual process will always remain the same.

You'll go on a farewell tour that's longer than your paper clip snake link. You'll walk down the halls, waving to all the Grinners and Late Stayers. You'll have a legitimate conversation with the mail guy, thanking him for looking the other way while you sent out personal letters and packages.

The IT guy will be in his closet office surrounded by computers. Maybe he'll be playing Atari. He'll pretend like he's stressed and busy, and you'll be out of there right after thanking him for letting you bypass the firewall to download music. The person who hates you will be in the hall, watching from a distance, waiting for you to leave, counting down the minutes with the Human Clock.

Jim in Marketing will shake your hand and say something insightful, Barbara in Human Resources won't know what to say, but as she fumbles for the proper words she'll come up with a politely awkward way to ask you for your keys and ID back. You'll feel like a cop in a bad movie who has to turn in his badge after making a lethal mistake. But of course the cop then finds the serial killer vigilante-style. This is what you have to do. Stay strong, don't show any weakness, promise to keep in touch, and get outta there as fast as you can. Time to start a new chapter.

Temping

Should you be unlucky enough to actually have to temp for a while—do a good job. Most temp agencies are crawling with freaks. Guys who dress like they are the lead singer in a rockabilly band, women who look like they just came in from riding the rails. Temps are usually struggling writers, artists, actors, or community college attendees who need to throw a little cash in their back packet.

Every once in a while you find a temp who is really good—and guess what? They get hired full time or at least get called back. There's nothing worse than getting a temp job and doing a bad job. Basically a temp job is a company giving you a trial period. If they like you, they'll want to find you something or bring you on board when the timing is right. Especially if you are nice, normal, smart, and competent. So don't screw it up by bringing your guitar and playing on your lunch break; don't listen to speed metal on your computer; don't argue with your boyfriend for thirty minutes on the phone.

Go to work, file what they want you to file, copy what they want you to copy, get someone to sign your temp time card, say thanks, and get out of there.

CHAPTER 16

MISCELLANEOUS

Corporate Seasons

AFTER YOU'VE BEEN WORKING FOR A WHILE, YOU'LL start to realize that time is now measured in seasons. Day in, day out, it's all the same monotony. The week begins, the week ends, "Damn, it's Monday again." "Thank God it's Friday!" The weeks are all the same and the only thing that is really any different is the pervading atmosphere. Seasons change the overall mood around the office, and here are some accurate generalizations to prepare for:

FALL: The dog days of summer have drawn to a close, there are no holidaze coming up, the kids are back at school, the parents are back at work full time. Aside from the leaves falling from the trees, fall feels like the Rebirth season.

Unfortunately, the Halloween Party is right around the corner. Find out if your company is the dressing-up type. Usually this happens if the bosses feel the need to "pick up morale." If this is the type of thing that's actually encouraged in your workplace, obviously you don't want to get *too* into it. Come up with something creative, even topical, that requires little effort to throw together. You don't want to give off the impression that you took leisure time away from the office and used it to make a costume. Use discretion, definitely no "sexy devil" or "naughty nurse" costumes, and don't ever wear a fake mustache or you'll look like a loser. Above all, don't wear anything too noticeable because then your coworkers will all want to talk to you about it; not to mention it sends the wrong message to upper management. You never know when you might be called into that unexpected meeting. It'll be hard to convince your clients that your company is up to the task at hand when you're explaining fourth-quarter profits dressed like Dracula.

WINTER: Everyone walks a step slower, and sometimes it's so cold, you actually don't mind being at the office. Unless you work outside. Winter's saving grace is the Christmas Spirit. For two weeks, everyone will be in a good mood. Gifts are given, pleasantries exchanged, affairs are consummated, and ignorant questions are asked about Chanukah. If your company is cool enough to give you time off during the time between Christmas and New Years, winter also boasts the longest holiday period of the year. Enjoy!

SPRING: The bipolar season. Sometimes it's more like winter; sometimes it's more like summer. The April/May period is generally a good time because the weather's finally starting to get warm. Finally something decent to talk about in the elevators. You'll hear things like, "Wow, it's such a beautiful day outside." "We should ask the boss if we can work outside today!"

April Fools' Day can get a little tricky. If you think there's a chance your little prank may cross any lines, it's probably better to resort to a less offensive joke that's more practical.

Spring is also the best time for wardrobes. The women look

beautiful in their newest DKNY, and maybe even the men will lay down their blue button-down shirts and khakis in favor of some different colors.

SUMMER: The best of the seasons, the office feels a little more laid back and the work days get shorter. Weather talk is cordial and coworkers start leaving earlier on Fridays. If it was a Friday in October, you wouldn't dare take off at 3 p.m.

Of course, none of this really matters. You spend all day inside anyway under bright fluorescent lights surrounded by monitored 68–72-degree temperature. The AC kicks on when the thermostat reads 72; the heat kicks on if it's lower than 68. Good times. So the fifth season of the year, by default, after summer, winter, spring, and fall is . . . Corporate! But unlike the other four seasons, you will never hear, "I can't wait for Corporate; it's definitely my favorite season." That's because it's always Corporate, all day . . . every day.

The Little Victories

They are what is truly important at work. Because the fact is, aside from a promotion, you won't get too many large victories. And it all depends on what you consider a large victory. For me, anything shy of a promotion falls short. That makes everything else a small victory. Stealing highlighters, getting two Cokes for the price of one out of the vending machine, a successful Geographic War. These are all small victories.

Once McDonald's was delivering lunch to a few of my office mates on a rainy day. When they arrived with only three Big Mac combos (instead of the three Big Mac combos and two milkshakes ordered) someone from my office called to complain. Next thing we knew, McDonald's accidentally redelivered the entire order . . . twice! So we had nine Big Mac combos and four milkshakes in the office. Word of the surplus McDonald's spread through the office like the gold rush of 1849. I remember people running through the hall to grab a handful of fries, or just maybe half of a Big Mac as if they had never had fast-food in their lives. Needless to say, it's pretty obvious that these people needed a lot of something—and that something, though not obvious to them, was not McDonalds.

Sometimes you'll need to create your own little victories, otherwise you won't end up with too much to cheer about at the office. Here's a great small victory that takes weeks, maybe even months, but when it's complete you will feel utter and total satisfaction: If you work in a high-rise or any sort of building where you have to flash a picture ID, occasionally there's that one guard who will pretend not to know you even if you've worked there for the past five years. Every morning the same shit, "Let me see your ID, please." "C'mon, man, I left it at home." "Go back to the front and get a pass." But if in the beginning of your tenure with him you flash him your ID with a little less visibility than those around you, he'll grow to know you as one of the guys who flashes it really quickly. Not quick enough so that he can't see, but just quickly enough so that he can and quicker than everyone else's.

Now do that trick for about a month. Then one day speed it up on him. Show the ID and pull it back quicker than you ever have. At first he'll want to say, "Let me see your ID," but a little spark in his brain will go off and remind him that you're one of the fast flashers and as usual you're just flashing your badge quickly. It won't register with him that you're doing it quicker than usual. Do that for a month. By your third month there you'll be flashing the badge quicker than anyone in the building, and he'll never stop you for a closer examination. You'll have established your territory in his world, and as long as the other 99.9 percent of employees obey his speed rules, you will get off without a hitch. A Little Victory.

You can find Little Victories everywhere if you look hard enough. Every now and then you'll have to talk to that guy who refuses to take his phone off speakerphone. He answers the phone on speakerphone, he talks on speakerphone, and he talks to others while he's talking to you on speakerphone. Sure this is a practical and accepted way of doing business, but it's obnoxious and you can never really hear the person on the other line. Speakerphone should never be tolerated unless, of course, it's your boss doing the talking.

When I'm talking to someone on speakerphone, I like to play Speakerphone Joust. I put my phone on speakerphone, too. Now I can't hear them and they can't hear me, and then it's just a matter of who moves first. Neither of you can do business until the other person budges. Usually they'll say, "Hold on a sec, I can't really hear you that well." And then they'll pick up the phone. Score one for the good guys.

What They Say vs. What They Mean

Your coworkers will often make statements that aren't true. These words cannot be considered lies because your coworkers are not really aware that they're lying when they make false statements. Compliments, suggestions, promises, plans, it's all relative in the Corporate World. It helps if you can pick up on a few choice buzzwords the moment you hear them. Save yourself some time in the long run by recognizing the real meaning of these ten commonly overheard Corporate Phrases:

1. "That would be great" *means,* "Go for it. I'm too lazy to do it myself, but feel free to go ahead and do it."
2. "Hmm, I can't really get to it at the moment, maybe you want to try Jim in Marketing?" *means,* "It's not something I usually do, therefore, I really don't want to do it right now. Or ever." Meaning, "No."

3. "How was your weekend?" *means,* "I'm setting you up to tell you about my weekend by graciously asking you about yours first, even though what I only want to do is tell you about mine."

4. "Good idea, let's discuss it first thing Monday morning" *means,* "Follow up with me next Wednesday."

5. "PCs are better than MACs" *means,* "I only use one side of my brain."

6. "MACs are better than PCs" *means,* "I pretend to know a lot about computers but all I really know is that there are two types of computers, and the commercials tell me which one to like."

7. "Can you please hold?" *means,* "You don't have a choice; the call on the other line is more important."

8. "Don't worry, she knows me" *means,* "She has no idea who I am but hopefully this little ruse will get her to pick up the phone."

9. "We should find a way to get it done a little quicker next time" *means,* "You should find a way to get it done a lot quicker next time or there won't be a next time."

10. "I needed it yesterday" *means,* "I forgot to tell you I needed this urgently, so now you're totally fucked."

Needless to say, if the person needed it "yesterday," they should have given it to you two days ago rather than two minutes ago.

Top Ten Things You Will Hate About the Corporate World

I don't have the space to write about them all . . . so here are ten!

10. Fluorescent lights: Look at them right now. You will be sitting under them for the next twenty-five years. Do you know why

these bulbs are used? Because they last longer than any other bulb on the market. Why? Because all day they're sucking life away from you to power themselves.

9. Loss of identity: You become Corporate. Over time you will dress like everyone else at the company. Your haircut will change, your style will change, your car, your music, your movies, your taste in food, and your sexual attractions—will all change due to your new environment when you spend 70 percent of your waking life in this new place.

8. Cubicles: Odds are pretty good you're going to start off in a cubicle. And that means the guy next to you is in a cubicle. And the woman next to him. And the guy next to her . . . It's a barren cubicle planet lit by an oppressive fluorescent sun.

7. Office lingo: Words like "Re:" and "FYI" will become part of your daily language. Get familiar with them, ASAP.

6. Bosses: You just spent the last four years of your life being your own boss. No parents, no principal—just liberal college professors who could care less about you as long as you did your work. Now you've got someone breathing down your neck again.

5. Early mornings: For the next twenty-five years you'll be up bright and early. You'd better eat your Wheaties.

4. Sitting: Sure you had to do it when you went to class. You do it for breakfast, lunch, and dinner. You do it to watch TV, play video games, primp yourself, and to drive. But class never lasted eight hours, and you can't sit around watching TV that long unless there's a *Beavis and Butt-head* marathon. Yet now you're expected to sit in front of a computer for eight hours a day. Maybe you get a couple of ten-minute breaks here and there, but they go faster than the Snickers in the vending machine.

3. Taxes: Just wait till you get your first paycheck. Wait till you see how much money they take out for taxes. It's unbelievable,

and you'll wonder where all the money goes. Then you'll read about the 17-trillion-dollar-satellite that broke in space and fell out of orbit. A NASA official will nerdily say, "Ooops," but he looks like he tried hard so no one will get mad; and we'll all complacently wait for the president to spoonfeed us a sound bite about the importance of space exploration. Important to whom? Who the fuck cares if a planet in some nebulous galaxy has some rings around it? Are you working where you are now because the local planetarium wasn't hiring? Personally, I'd rather have my money back.

2. The devil's advocate: You're in charge of making your own decisions, but sometimes we all doubt our choices and question our motives. At times you'll be filled with doubt about the path you chose. Am I in the right place? Did I choose the right company? Is this job really secure? Should I have stuck around campus and played guitar in the Coffee Shop?

1. Oh shit, here comes my boss. Time to minimize!

CHAPTER 17

THE END OF THE BEGINNING

I HOPE THIS READ DIDN'T MAKE YOU TOO miserable. I hope I didn't paint a horrible picture. The fact is, work CAN open many doors into the opportunities of life. You might meet your future spouse through work, who could eventually mother or father your child. You might find that you've got an undiscovered talent you would never have realized. You have to work. It's that simple. Unless you're a trust fund kid—you have to work.

Hopefully this book turned you into an expert on everything Corporate. You will now hold on to your identity and do a great job at the office. You'll never look forward to the season "Corporate," and you'll never become that person who nauseated you on your First Day. Don't play the Name Game and don't subject the newbie to the Corporate Initiation Test. Let others find out where they're from, who hired them, their salary. If you start playing the Name Game, all hope is lost and this book has done you no good.

Now that you've seen what it takes to make it in the Corporate World, you've got to give yourself the tools to succeed. You must put up your own defense mechanisms against those things that will try to bring you down. Display a positive Corporate Identity during business hours, but use the Corey Hart theory at night. Be rebellious when possible. Trust me, whatever rebellious act you do once you're in the Corporate World won't come anywhere close to your rebellious teen or college days, but being young and having fun whenever possible will help defend against the physical and mental atrophy that can and will set in after a year on the job.

If you work, you are not "cool." There is no way in hell that you can be cool, no matter what kind of music you listen to, no matter what kind of clothes you wear, and no matter what kind of car you drive. It's that simple. The eighteen-year-old version of you was a lot more fun, a lot more hip, and a lot more cool. So whenever possible, step outside of your Corporate self and do whatever the eighteen-year-old version of you would have done. But this time, put your seat belt on.

On that same note, get to the gym at least twice a week. Work your heart on the treadmill; work your biceps on the Nautilus. Stretch, do some sit-ups, stare at yourself in the mirror (it's good for confidence), and then get a power smoothie. Hit the sauna, the showers, and head home. You're older now. You've got to this if you're going to last. Of course, if you didn't have to work, you'd have no mental or physical stress. You'd live to be a hundred with your eyes closed.

But that's just it—your eyes would be closed. Working opens up your eyes to a world of opportunities and experiences. The trick is to not fall into the traps along the way. Your boss is going to throw everything at you; and in the end, only the strongest will get promoted. Eating healthy, exercising regularly, having good friends, relaxing, taking a step back, being friendly, dressing nicely, taking care of yourself—these are subtle ways to stay ahead of the pack.

The rest will just shake your hand on your way to your corner office with the picture windows. Which, may I add, has a great view of the outside world. And once you can view the outside world, you are one step closer to getting there.

I do want to share one final story of how my misery affected me. It was a misery that I felt just weeks removed from college, when I moved into a new apartment, in a new city, three thousand miles away from a coast I had called home my entire life. It's in this misery that you find yourself wishing for hateful things to happen. I have to admit that in a sick sort of way there is a tiny, tiny portion of me that wishes bad things would happen, causing us not to have to go to work. Usually it would be blizzards or snow storms, but now living in New York City I quickly see that unless it snows twelve inches or more—we're still marching to work, transportation or no transportation.

I want a blizzard. A tornado. A natural disaster that'll rip up the city. When I lived in Los Angeles, I used to stand on my deck and pray to the Earthquake gods, "Earthquake gods, strike in the middle of the night! Bring down those telephone poles! Disrupt that highway! Mr. Earthquake, tear down those walls!" I used to imagine the chaos; it was beautiful. I prayed that every time I heard a car alarm it was a preshock of something better to come. The Big One. The one that would cancel work for days until running water, electricity, and the infrastructure could be restored. Even then, only some of the workers would be able to show up, and it would be like those old snow days in school when only half the student body and teachers showed up and you kind of just hung out and talked about current events and issues that mattered. Funny, those are the days I remember most.

Remember the Great Blackout of 2003? At first everyone's instinct in the Northeast was to freak out. Terrorism? Sabotage? Earthquake? OK, regain composure, grab your personal belongings, and head to the nearest exit.

Out on the street, everyone was curious. What had happened? Personally, I didn't care! It was 4 p.m. and I was out of work! On a Thursday! And I had just heard on the radio it wasn't terrorism and no one was hurt and no major catastrophe had occurred. Everything was intact and spirits were high. Why? Well, EVERY-ONE knew that power wasn't going to be restored by the next day. People, New Yorkers especially, know these things. So what else to do but party! People were running around in the streets; others were drinking in pitch-black bars where they were charging $10 for a Coors Lite!

On the Friday of the Great Blackout of 2003, 50 million people found themselves without electricity. No phone, no air-conditioning, no real food, no ice, no cell phones, no lights, no TV, no radio. But most importantly, no work! If you were one of those people, ask yourself—was that Friday not one of the greatest days ever? I was sweating my ass off sitting in my apartment with no air-conditioning in 95-degree heat. I cringed at the thought of eating another Snack-well cookie for lunch. I longed for an ice water. But it was all a thousand times better than sitting in my cubicle fielding questions like, "Doin' anything fun this weekend? My husband and I are heading up to the Adirondacks to go camping. I love camping . . ." Four and a half years after accepting my first corporate job, my prayers had been answered in the form of a blackout. It was a Snow Day for adults.

Nobody wants to be confined in an office. You don't want to be at the place where you spend forty to fifty hours a week. You don't want to be with the people that you endure forty to fifty hours a week with. You don't find the chair comfortable, you don't find the work challenging, you don't like your boss, you don't like your pay. . . . And yet, quite possibly—you will be doing this for the next 40 years of your life. Enjoy!

Well? What did you think? Are you glad you graduated? Do you think you can handle eating lunch at your desk surrounded by people who are going to comment on how bad it smells? Do you know how to use the copy machine? Can you fax? Are you organized? Can you use Microsoft Excel? How are your phone manners? Do you mind never having time to exercise any more? Maybe you've found the preceding pages as a foreshadowing for challenges to come. Maybe the thought of working an entire year and ending up with $500 or working a whole year and hanging out with people that you dislike didn't sit well with you. If this is the case, I do have one final piece of advice. Go to Grad School!

ACKNOWLEDGMENTS

The authors would like to thank the following people for their valuable contributions. Without them, this book would suck.

Phil Altmann
David Embree
Nancy Embree
Alyssa Embree
Katie Furlong
George Garrett
Robyn "The Maven" Gunn
Matt Heller
Scott "Agent Extraordinaire" Hoffman
Erica Korman
Stefanie Lindskog
Peter Miller
NA English Department

ACKNOWLEDGMENTS

Lisa Shapiro
Price Shapiro
Rand Shapiro
Jennifer Weis